Ruthless!
THE MUSICAL

BOOK & LYRICS BY
JOEL PALEY

MUSIC BY
MARVIN LAIRD

SAMUEL FRENCH, INC.
45 WEST 25TH STREET   NEW YORK 10010
7623 SUNSET BOULEVARD   HOLLYWOOD 90046
LONDON   TORONTO

Copyright © 1995 by Joel Paley (book) and Nohners Music (lyrics)

ALL RIGHTS RESERVED

Amateurs wishing to arrange for the production of RUTHLESS! must make application to SAMUEL FRENCH, INC., at 45 West 25th Street, New York, NY 10010, giving the following particulars:

> (1) The name of the town and theatre or hall of the proposed production.
> (2) The maximum seating capacity of the theatre or hall.
> (3) Scale of ticket prices.
> (4) The number of performances intended and the dates thereof.
> (5) Indicate whether you will use an orchestration or simply a piano.

Upon receipt of these particulars SAMUEL FRENCH, INC., will quote terms and availability.

Stock royalty quoted on application to SAMUEL FRENCH, INC., 45 West 25th Street, New York, NY 10010.

For all other rights than those stipulated above, apply to Samuel French, Inc., 45 W. 25th Street, New York, NY 10010.

An orchestration consisting of
Piano 1/Conductor's Score
Piano 2
Percussion
Bass

will be loaned two months prior to the production ONLY on receipt of the royalty quoted for all performances, the rental fee and a refundable deposit. The deposit will be refunded on the safe return to SAMUEL FRENCH, INC. of all materials loaned for the production.

No one shall commit or authorize any act or omission by which the copyright of, or the right to copyright, this play may be impaired.

No one shall make any changes in this play for the purpose of production.

Publication of this play does not imply availability for performance. Both amateurs and professionals considering a production are *strongly* advised in their own interests to apply to Samuel French, Inc., for written permission before starting rehearsals, advertising, or booking a theatre.

No part of this book may be reproduced, stored in a retrieval system, or transmitted in any form, by any means, now known or yet to be invented, including mechanical, electronic, photocopying, recording, videotaping, or otherwise, without the prior written permission of the publisher.

Printed in the U.S.A.
ISBN 0 573 69525-3

"Have I Stayed Too Long at the Fair" Music & Lyrics © 1956, 1957 by Tylerson Music Co., Inc. Used by permission.

For permission to use the Connie Francis recording of "Who's Sorry Now?" please contact Mills Music, Inc., 810 Seventh Ave., 36th floor, New York, NY 10019 and Ted Snyder Music, P.O. Box 2327, Palm Desert, CA 92260.

IMPORTANT BILLING AND CREDIT REQUIREMENTS

All producers of RUTHLESS! *must* give credit to the Authors of the Work in all programs distributed in connection with performances of the Work, and in all instances in which the title of the Work appears for the purposes of advertising, publicizing or otherwise exploiting a production thereof; including, without limitation, to programs, souvenir books and playbills. The names of the Authors *must* also appear on a separate line in which no other matter appears, immediately following the title of the Work, and *must* be in size of type not less than 50% of the size of type used for the title of the Work.

The size, type, prominence, boldness and color of said "Theatre Works" credit shall be no less than seventy-five percent (75%) of the smalles credit accorded either the costume, lighting or scenic designer of said production.

Billing *must* be substantially as follows:

(Name of Producer)

presents

RUTHLESS!
The Musical

Book and Lyrics by   Music by
Joel Paley   Marvin Laird

Originally produced by Musical Theatre Works, Inc.
Anthony J. Stimac, Executive Director

Produced Off-Broadway in New York City by
Kim Lang Lenny, Wolfgang Bocksch and Jim Lenny

/ / /

The author wishes to dedicate this script to the premiere companies of "Ruthless!" whose unique contributions provided many of the laughs on these pages.

And to Jim Merillat and Laura Anderson at Samuel French. Thank you.

PRODUCTION HISTORY

Players Theatre, New York City
Opening Night: May 6, 1992

Sylvia St. Croix	Joel Vig
Judy Denmark	Donna English
Tina Denmark	Laura Bundy
Myrna Thorn	Susan Mansur
Louise Lerman	Joanne Baum
Lita Encore	Denise Lor
Eve	Joanne Baum
Emily Block	Susan Mansur

Directed by Joel Paley
Musical Direction by Marvin Laird
Scenery by James Noone
Costumes by Gail Cooper-Hecht
Lighting by Kenneth Possner
Sound by Tom Source
Production Stage Manager: Pam Edington

Candlelight's Forum Theatre, Chicago
Oepning Night: January 20, 1993

Sylvia St. Croix	Dale Benson
Judy Denmark	Paula Scrofano
Tina Denmark	Priscilla Behne
Myrna Thorn	E. Faye Butler
Louise Lerman	Nicole Losurdo
Lita Encore	Renee Matthews
Eve	Catherine Lord
Emily Block	Aleshia Brevard

Directed by Joel Paley
Musical Direction by Nick Vendon
Scenery by James Noone
Costumes by Gail Cooper-Hecht
Lighting by Kenneth Possner
Sound by David Pomatto
Production Stage Manager: Billy Carey

Canon Theatre, Beverly Hills
Opening Night: October 15, 1993

Sylvia St. Croix	Loren Freeman
Judy Denmark	Joan Ryan
Tina Denmark	Lindsay Ridgeway
Myrna Thorn	Nancy Linari
Louise Lerman	Joanne Baum
Lita Encore	Rita McKenzie
Eve	Joanne Baum
Emily Block	Nancy Linari

Directed by Joel Paley
Musical Direction by Nick Vendon
Scenery by Lawrence Miller
Costumes by Bob Mackie
Lighting by Michael Gilliam
Sound by Michael C. Cousins
Production Stage Manager: Kathleen Horton

AUTHOR'S NOTES

STYLE
Ruthless! is a musical farce, fast and furious, with well-timed entrances and exits. The pace should be driven. Dramatic pauses are few and far between and carefully chosen. The audience must never get ahead of the wordplay or the action. Emotional transitions should be abrupt and sharp. These characters never miss a beat. Above all, the actors must take the situations ultra-seriously. They are not aware of the jokes they are making. There should be no winking at the audience, so to speak.

PREPARATION
I recommend the Director, Musical Director, Actors and all Production Designers watch the following films prior to rehearsals, as *Ruthless!* parodies their styles and attitudes. Though it is not necessary for the audience to be familiar with the source material being parodied, the creative team should know specifically what they are sending up. The films are:

The Bad Seed — Parody of melodramatic plot, old-fashioned values, and over the top histrionics.
All About Eve — Parody of plot and attitudes. (The candy dish sequence is a direct visual quote.)
Gypsy — The shifting of power, mother/daughter relationships, and stage mothers, in general.
The Women — Overall pacing and style. The quick and pointed dialogue.
Valley of the Dolls — Cliché attitudes towards show business.

All are available on video and highly recommended.

TIME PERIOD
Although the show takes place in the present, it should have a distinct "fifties" feel, reflecting the family values of a more innocent time. The glamour of Act II should also have a retro-style that reflects the "sixties" Hollywood cliché take on showbiz success.

CASTING
There are nine characters, including "Frederick" who appears only at the very end and delivers the show's final line. It's a good idea to have an ASM who can play the part. In the past, local guest stars were used. (This role should not be credited in the program as it is a surprise.) As far as the eight female characters: They can be performed by six to eight actors with some doubling up. For instance, Miss Thorn (Act I) can double as Miss Block (Act II) and Louise (Act I) can play Eve (Act II). Or Miss Thorn can play Eve and Louise can double as Miss Block. It all depends on your actors' particular strengths. If casting one actor per role, a child can be used to play Louise.

Traditionally, Sylvia St. Croix has been played by a man, with marvelous results. The show can be cast with any combination of men and women, but if casting a man in any of the roles, the actor should perform the role "straight," and not over-play the drag aspect. You want the audience to laugh at the character as opposed to laughing at a man in a dress.

Needless to say, the younger the actress playing Tina, the more outrageous the effect. If an adult actor is used, she (or he) must play the role honestly as a child.

MISCELLANEOUS
Note about Judy Denmark: There must be no hint of Ginger DelMarco in Judy until late in Act I. We must come to believe Judy is not capable of the outrageous

behavior she displays in the second act. Her performance should be a steady build in Act I peaking with "I'm a talented girl, Mama!"

The Act II prologue, (montage), should be staged in front of the show curtain so as not to reveal the Act II set. The actors should be revealed one at a time in a pool of light.

If you have any questions please write to me care of:

Rosenstone/Wender
3 East 48th Street, 4th floor
New York, NY 10017

Have a ball!

Joel Paley

PROLOGUE

(Music Cue 1: PROLOGUE)

SYLVIA. Talent! Where does it come from? Good evening. My name is Sylvia St. Croix. Where does talent come from? Is it a product of environment, something you pick up off the street? Or is talent something you're born with, something passed down from generation to generation, something in the blood? I wonder. Meet Judy Denmark.

(The curtain parts. JUDY is carrying a breakfast tray of toast and coffee. SHE poses.)

SYLVIA. Pretty, isn't she?

(JUDY sets the tray on the coffee table, sits on the sofa, and pours a cup of coffee.)

SYLVIA. A wife and mother leading an idyllic suburban life. And although Judy has absolutely no talent whatsoever, her only child, her daughter, Tina, has been blessed with a great deal of talent. Blessed...or dare I say cursed! (*Laughs.*) But I'm getting ahead of myself.

(SYLVIA points to the telephone. It RINGS. SHE laughs and exits.)

SCENE 1:
THE DENMARK LIVING ROOM – MORNING.

(Music Cue 2: TINA'S MOTHER)

JUDY. I'll get it.

(PHONE rings again. JUDY answers.)

JUDY.
HELLO?
YES, THIS IS TINA'S MOTHER
HELLO, MRS. PETERS
HOW'S THAT?
TINA BROUGHT YOU FLOWERS FROM OUR GARDEN?
YES, SHE'S A SPECIAL GIRL
WE'RE VERY PROUD OF HER
THANK YOU FOR CALLING
GOOD-BYE

(Hangs up. PHONE rings.)

I'll get it. *(SHE answers.)*

HELLO?
YES, THIS IS TINA'S MOTHER
HELLO, MRS. MILLER
HOW'S THAT?
TINA HELPED YOU DO A LOAD OF LAUNDRY?
WELL SHE'S SO FOND OF YOU.
SHE LIKES YOUR HUSBAND TOO!
THANK YOU FOR CALLING

GOOD-BYE

(Hangs up. PHONE rings. SHE answers.)

TINA'S MOTHER HERE
HI, MRS. ADAMS
A PARTY?
I'LL TELL HER SHE'S INVITED

(Hangs up. PHONE rings. SHE answers.)

TINA'S MOTHER HERE
SORRY, MRS. ADAMS
THAT SATURDAY AT FOUR?
I'M SURE SHE'LL BE DELIGHTED
BYE

(Hangs up.)

I COULD HAVE BEEN AN OFFICE GIRL
A WIZARD AT DICTATION
WORKING FIFTY WEEKS A YEAR
TWO WEEKS PAID VACATION
I COULD HAVE BEEN A TEACHER
TEACHING ONE THING OR ANOTHER
BUT I'M PROUD TO BE WHAT I AM
TINA'S MOTHER!

(PHONE RINGS. SHE answers.)

HELLO?
YES, THIS IS TINA'S MOTHER
HELLO, MRS. FARMER
HOW'S THAT?
TINA SANG A SONG TO YOUR BLIND MOTHER?
SHE'S SO COMPASSIONATE
AND SO DARN TALENTED
AND THAT'S THE HALF OF IT

HER ROOM IS ALWAYS NEAT
I THANK MY LUCKY STARS
SHE'S POSITIVELY HEAVEN-SENT
MY KID'S THE PERFECT EIGHT-YEAR-OLD
YES, SHE'S ENTHRALLING
THANK YOU FOR CALLING
GOOD-BYE

(Hangs up. DOORBELL.)

I'll get it. *(Picks up the phone.)*
HELLO? HELLO?

(DOORBELL.)

Hello??

(DOORBELL. Realizing it's the door, SHE hangs up, floats to the front door and opens it. SYLVIA ST. CROIX enters wearing dark glasses.)

SYLVIA. Mrs. Denmark? Mrs. Judy Denmark?
JUDY. Why, yes, I'm Judy. I'm Judy Denmark. Judy Denmark. That's my name. Judy. Judy Denmark.
SYLVIA. Tina's mother?
JUDY. *(Sung.)*
THAT'S ME!
SYLVIA. My card. *(Hands JUDY a card.)*
JUDY. I'm afraid mine are being printed. Won't you come in ... *(Reads card.)* ... Miss St. Croix.
SYLVIA. Please, call me Sylvia.
JUDY. Sylvia St. Croix. Are you French?
SYLVIA. St. Croix is a stage name.
JUDY. Ahh.
SYLVIA. My real name is Sylvia St. Sidney.
JUDY. Oh.
SYLVIA. Need I say more?
JUDY. Uh-uh.

(SYLVIA removes her glasses and looks around.)

SYLVIA. My, what a lovely home.
JUDY. Thank you, Sylvia.
SYLVIA. Beautiful curtains.
JUDY. Thank you, Sylvia.
SYLVIA. That's a smart dress.
JUDY. Thank you, Sylvia.

(SYLVIA eyes Judy's breakfast.)

SYLVIA. And mmm mmm mmm, doesn't this look delicious.
JUDY. It's toast, Sylvia.
SYLVIA. Denmark. Denmark. What sort of name is Denmark?
JUDY. I'm not sure ... Danish?
SYLVIA. No, thanks, the toast is fine. (*Snatches a piece of toast.*) Is your husband at home?
JUDY. (*Calls off-stage.*) Frederick?? (*Long pause.*) I'm afraid not.
SYLVIA. Working?
JUDY. I hope so.
SYLVIA. Pity. I do so like speaking with both parents. When will Mr. Denmark be returning?
JUDY. Could be any minute.
SYLVIA. Oh.
JUDY. Or a couple of days ...
SYLVIA. Oh, dear.
JUDY. A week ...
SYLVIA. A week?
JUDY. A month ...
SYLVIA. A month?
JUDY. Hard to say. He's a very busy man.
SYLVIA. What does Mr. Denmark do? (*JUDY shrugs.*) Well, whatever it is, you must be terribly proud of him.

JUDY. Uh-huh.
SYLVIA. You're a very luck girl, Judy Denmark.
JUDY. I know ... I'm a libra.
SYLVIA. This gorgeous home, a successful husband, whatever it is he does. (*Bites toast.*) Good toast! And of course the very reason I'm here ... your daughter, Tina. (Music Cue 2A: BEFORE "BORN TO ENTERTAIN") I caught her performance at the Rolling Hills Twilight Home for the Elderly. Sensational!
JUDY. We're very proud of our daughter.
SYLVIA. It was a triumph.
JUDY. If you like, I could arrange for her to perform for all of you again next Saturday.

(*SYLVIA chokes on toast.*)

SYLVIA. I don't live there, Mrs. Denmark. I was visiting an elderly friend.
JUDY. Sorry.
SYLVIA. Now then, about Tina ...?
JUDY. Would you like to meet her?
SYLVIA. I'd love to.
JUDY. I'll call her. She's out in the garage breaking in her new tap shoes. (Music Cue 3: BORN TO ENTERTAIN) (*Calling out window.*) Tina! You're on!

(*JUDY opens the door and stands back. TINA DENMARK bursts on stage wearing tap shoes.*)

TINA. Hello, Mother.
JUDY. Tina, we have company.
TINA. (*Strikes pose.*) I love company.
JUDY. Darling, say hello to Miss St. Croix.

(*TINA does a dance break.*)

TINA. Hi!
JUDY. Tina loves to perform.

TINA.
SOME GIRLS LIKE TO COOK AND SEW
WHEN I COOK IT'S IN A SHOW
I WAS BORN TO ENTERTAIN

(To audience.)

How ya doin'?

SOME GIRLS PREFER TO HELP MOM CLEAN
I'D RATHER LEARN A DANCE ROUTINE
I WAS BORN TO ENTERTAIN

Where ya from?

INSTEAD OF WALKIN' I GO FLAPPIN'
WHEN I TAP I MAKE IT HAPPEN
MOM SAYS I HAVE BROADWAY ON THE BRAIN
DON'T GET TOO COMFY IN THAT SEAT
WHEN I STRUT MY STUFF
YOU'LL BE ON YOUR FEET
I WAS BORN TO SING AND DANCE

(TINA runs to SYLVIA, who whirls her around and stands her on the coffee table, as JUDY, in the nick of time, clears the breakfast tray.)

Break!

(SHE taps.)

SYLVIA. Sell it, sweetheart!
TINA.
NOT EVERY SHOW-BIZ CINDERELLA
HAS GOT TO COME FROM POCATELLA
MY STAR WILL RISE LIKE BUBBLES IN CHAMPAGNE
BY NOW YOU'VE GUESSED MY ONE AMBITION

IT'S NOT TO BE NO MATHEMATICIAN

I WAS BORN TO AMUSE
FROM THE TIP OF MY NOSE
TO THE TAP OF MY SHOES
SO STRIKE UP THE BAND
AND HAND ME MY HAT AND MY CANE
'CAUSE I WAS BORN TO ENTERTAIN!

(JUDY grabs a can of Pledge and wipes off the coffee table. TINA sits on the sofa. JUDY wipes the soles of her shoes.)

SYLVIA. Bravo! That was brilliant, dear. Bravo!
TINA. Thank you, Madame St. Croix.
SYLVIA. Please, call me Sylvia.
TINA. Alright, Sylvia. *(To JUDY.)* Judy?
JUDY. That was very good, Tina, and, please, call me Mommy.
SYLVIA. Tina, how would you like to be a star?

(Music Cue 3A: AFTER "BORN TO ENTERTAIN")

TINA. Why, it's all I've ever wanted. *(Stands on coffee table.)* More than anything in the whole wide world.

(JUDY lifts her off.)

SYLVIA. Well, that's why I'm here. I work with specially gifted children. I plan careers as well as develop talent. Let me be frank. I think little Tina here can be big. You are planning a theatrical career for your daughter, are you not?
JUDY. We want her to finish school first.
SYLVIA. Of course. What time does she get out? *(Looks at watch.)* Three?
JUDY. I wasn't just talking about today.

SYLVIA. Oh.
JUDY. We want our daughter to have a normal childhood.
TINA. I've had a normal childhood. It's time to move on.
JUDY. So few make it in show business, sweetheart.
SYLVIA. But your daughter's good, Mrs. Denmark, and with my help she can be great.
JUDY. I still think it's important that she finish her formal education. I want her to have something to fall back on.
SYLVIA. And that's just what she'll do, the moment the going gets tough.
JUDY. Oh, but I ...
SYLVIA. I firmly believe, if you've nothing to fall back on, you simply don't fall back.
TINA. Makes sense.
SYLVIA. Whadda ya say?
TINA. Oh, Mama, say yes. Please say yes. I want to be good.
JUDY. You are good, baby.
TINA. I want to be gooder.
JUDY. I really think she should stay in school. Besides, childhood is a time for playing with dolls and riding a bike.

(Music Cue 4: TALENT)

SYLVIA.
OH, ANY TIKE CAN RIDE A BIKE
ANY BRAT CAN SWING A BAT
EVERY MOTHER'S CHILD PLAYS WITH BLOCKS
THEY RUN AND SKIP AND JUMP
AND CLIMB ON ROCKS
THAT MAY BE TRUE FOR EVERY DICK AND JANE
BUT SOME OF US WERE BORN TO ENTERTAIN ...

(JUDY and TINA freeze as SYLVIA vows.)

This time I'm doing it for you, baby!

(THEY unfreeze. SYLVIA sings to TINA.)

YOU CAN HAVE IT ALL—YOU'VE GOT TALENT
LIFE CAN BE A BALL IF YOU'VE GOT TALENT
WHEN IT'S OBVIOUS YOUR CHILD'S NOT
AN AVERAGE ORDINARY TOT
SHOWER HER WITH LOVE AND VALIDATION
JUDY, RECOGNIZE HER SPECIALTIES
CELEBRATE THE FACT THAT SHE'S
DESTINED TO A LIFE
A LIFE OF ADORATION

(To TINA.)

Come 'ere!

YOU'RE BETTER THAN THE REST
YOU'VE GOT TALENT
YOU WON'T HAVE TO GET UNDRESSED
IF YOU'VE GOT TALENT
YOU'RE NO SILLY PLASTIC INGENUE
IN CHEESY ADS FOR BRECK SHAMPOO
REALLY YOU'RE TOO GOOD FOR TELEVISION
   TINA. Really?
   SYLVIA. Really.
I'M TALKIN' STRAIGHT LEGIT, I MEAN
THE BROADWAY STAGE THE SILVER SCREEN!
BUT FIRST WE NEED YOUR MAMA
TO MAKE THE RIGHT DECISION
   TINA. Oh, Mama, please ...!
   SYLVIA. I'm not asking for a penny. Not a penny ... up front. Just a smallish percentage of her earnings.
   JUDY/TINA. How smallish?
   SYLVIA. That's something we should discuss in private.

TINA. We can go to my room.

(SYLVIA laughs.)

JUDY. I believe Sylvia was talking to Mommy, sweetheart. *(SYLVIA and TINA stare at her.)* You were talking to Mommy, weren't you?
SYLVIA. I'm sure we can work out all the meddlesome details. The important thing is to get started. She's not getting any younger, you know.
TINA. Please ...!
JUDY. Well, I suppose some coaching can't hurt. But only after school.
SYLVIA. We start this afternoon!
JUDY. I'm afraid she can't this afternoon.
TINA. Today's the audition for the school show.
SYLVIA. An audition?
TINA. I'm trying out for the lead.
SYLVIA. Then I want you to have this for luck. *(SHE takes a ring off her finger and gives it to TINA.)* This ring was given to me when I was a little girl starring in my school show.
TINA. Oh, it isn't brand new?
JUDY. It's better than new, sweetheart, it's an antique. *(SYLVIA reacts.)* Sorry. Tina, don't you have something to say to Sylvia?
TINA. Anything else for me?
SYLVIA. Well, you're not getting these. *(Indicates pearls.)* How 'bout some cash?
TINA. Fine.

(SYLVIA gives TINA money.)

JUDY. Really, Sylvia, you're too good to her.
SYLVIA. Oh, pish.
JUDY. Don't you have any children?
SYLVIA. *(Darkly.)* I prefer not to discuss it, Mrs. Denmark.

JUDY. I see.
SYLVIA. Let's just say she didn't have any talent.
JUDY. I'm so sorry.
SYLVIA. Not what I call talent! Oh, she used to jump around the living room. "Look, Mama, I'm dancing." But she was merely jumping. God, it was embarrassing.

(To TINA.)

YOU'LL NEVER HAVE TO HIDE
NO, YOU'VE GOT TALENT
AND I'LL BE BY YOUR SIDE TO GUIDE THAT
  TALENT
SO KICK UP YOUR HEELS AND TAP YOUR TOES
I'M YOUR AUNTIE MAME! YOUR MAMA ROSE!
AND NOTHING'S GONNA STOP US
'TIL WE'RE THROUGH
HONEY
SYLVIA WILL MAKE YOUR DREAM COME TRUE

YOU'VE GOT TALENT
LOTS OF TALENT
BABY, YOU'LL HAVE IT ALL
WAIT AND SEE
FOR ALONG WITH ALL THAT TALENT
YOU'VE GOT ...

(SHE catches Judy's eye.)

  ... your mother!

JUDY. Thank you.
SYLVIA.
AND ME!

(Music Cue 4A: TALENT – PLAYOFF)

RUTHLESS! 23

SCENE 2:
THE TURNER SCHOOL AUDITORIUM –
LATER THAT AFTERNOON

In the DARK we hear the following:

MISS THORN. Children, please proceed to the auditorium, the auditions for the school show are about to begin. No pushing. You will all be seen.

(LIGHTS UP. TINA, holding her picture and resume is standing among a row of cardboard cut-out children, à la "Chorus Line." MISS THORN addresses the audience.)

MISS THORN. People, people ... *(Clicks CLICKER for attention.)* Good afternoon, children, and welcome parents. I'm Miss Thorn, and, once again, based on my professional experience in "the show business," I am to have the honor of directing this year's school show ... "Pippi in Tahiti," the musical, by Myrna Thorn ... thank you.

(THORN freezes in time as TINA sings her thoughts.)

(Music Cue 5: TO PLAY THIS PART)

TINA.
TO DANCE MY DANCES
TO SING MY SONG
IT'S ALL I'VE WANTED
ALL I'VE DREAMED
MY WHOLE LIFE LONG
THO' I'M ONLY EIGHT YEARS OLD
JUST A BABY, SO I'M TOLD
CAN I HELP IT?

I ALREADY KNOW MY HEART
AND I'LL DO ANYTHING
TO PLAY THIS PART

MISS THORN. Let's begin, shall we? *(Calls TINA over and takes her picture and resume.)* Please welcome a multi-talented third grader—Miss Tina Denmark. *(Under her breath.)* Your best sixteen bars and off, dear.

TINA.
THE MERRY-GO-ROUND
IS BEGINNING TO SLOW NOW
HAVE I STAYED TOO LONG AT THE FAIR?
THE MUSIC HAS STOPPED ...

(TINA pauses dramatically. A confused MISS THORN approaches her. Suddenly, TINA belts out the next line, startling MISS THORN.)

TINA.
AND THE CHILDREN MUST GO NOW
HAVE I STAYED TOO LONG AT THE ...

(MISS THORN cuts her off.)

MISS THORN. Thank you! Bobby, teach her the ballet combination.
TINA. I already learned it in the hall.

(TINA dances a short ballet combination.)

MISS THORN. Jazz.
TINA. A five-six-seven-eight!

(TINA dances a jazz combination.)

MISS THORN. Interpretive.

(TINA does an interpretive dance.)

MISS THORN. That was Tina Denmark. Thank you, Tina. And now, please welcome ...

(LIGHTS OUT on MISS THORN as TINA sings her thoughts.)

TINA.
IF I SOUND DESPERATE
WELL IT'S BECAUSE
ALL I WANT
NO!
ALL I NEED
IS YOUR APPLAUSE
SO I PRAY TO HIM ON HIGH
THE CASTING AGENT IN THE SKY
CAST ME!
AND I'LL STAY TRUE TO MY ART
I'LL DO ANYTHING YOU PLEASE
POUND ERASERS ON MY KNEES
I'LL DO ANYTHING TO PLAY THIS PART

BLACKOUT

(When LIGHTS restore, MISS THORN is standing center stage, holding a huge stack of pictures and resumes. TINA stands among the "children.")

MISS THORN. I want to thank all of our talented students, and some of our not so talented ones. Really, Rachel Hobbs, what on earth were you doing? Before I announce the winner, I want to say a special thank you to Mike Lerman and Lerman's Hardware for donating all the paint and wood to build our lovely sets. Also, for supplying all the patterns and materials to make our gorgeous costumes, a very special thanks goes out to Betty Lerman and all the gals down at Betty's Needle Nook. Thank you, Betty. And now, ladies and gentlemen, boys and girls, the star of this year's school show ... (*TINA steps forward.*) ... Miss Louise Lerman!

(*LOUISE bursts through the curtain and bows center stage. The GIRLS stare at each other.*)

BLACKOUT

SCENE 3:
THE DENMARK LIVING ROOM – LATER THAT DAY.

TINA, depressed, sits on the sofa, staring at the ceiling.

SYLVIA. You had your heart set on playing Pippi, didn't you?
TINA. It's the title role.
JUDY. Tina ...
TINA. It's the best part in the show.
JUDY. Sweetheart ...
TINA. I don't understand. That Lerman girl's too Jewish-looking to play Pippi.
JUDY. Tina ...!
SYLVIA. She has no fire! No music!
JUDY. Darling, these things happen.
TINA. Not to me they don't.
SYLVIA. Atta girl!
JUDY. Please, Sylvia, I'll handle this. (*To TINA.*) And so what if Louise Lerman's playing Pippi. You get to play Puddles!
TINA. I don't want to play a dog.
SYLVIA. Puddles doesn't sing. Puddles doesn't even talk. Puddles is a stupid mime part.
TINA. I hate mime.
SYLVIA. Everyone does.
TINA. I mean, would you look at me. I was born to play Pippi Longstocking! I am Pippi Longstocking!

JUDY. That's enough, Tina.
TINA. Oh, I hate Louise Lerman! (*Stomps her feet.*)
JUDY. Now you listen to me, young lady, do you want to stay in show business?
TINA. You're right, Mother. (*Hugs JUDY.*) I just wanted that silly old part so you and Daddy would be proud of me.
JUDY. But we are proud of you, sweetheart. Of course, if you had gotten the part we would have been real, real proud, but nevertheless ...
TINA. Oh, Mother, what would you give me for a bucket o' kisses?
JUDY. Why, I'd give you a tub o' hugs.

(DOORBELL.)

TINA. I'll get it.

(Music Cue 5A: MISS THORN'S ENTRANCE)

(TINA opens the door. A wary MISS THORN enters.)

TINA. Why, good afternoon, Miss Thorn.
MISS THORN. Good afternoon, Tina. You're looking very pretty today.
TINA. Why, thank you, Miss Thorn. (*SHE curtsies.*)
MISS THORN. That was an excellent curtsy.
TINA. (*Another curtsy.*) Why, thank you, Miss Thorn.
MISS THORN. (*To JUDY.*) She's so polite.
JUDY. (*Curtsies.*) Why thank you, Miss Thorn.
MISS THORN. And I see where she gets it from.
TINA/JUDY. (*Curtsy together.*) Why, thank you, Miss Thorn.
JUDY. Run along, sweetheart, Mommy wants to talk to Miss Thorn.
TINA. (*Sweetly.*) Haven't changed your mind, have you?

MISS THORN. I'm afraid not.
TINA. (*Sharply.*) Come on, Sylvia. (*TINA storms out.*)
JUDY. Please, won't you sit down.
SYLVIA. Excuse me, Miss Thorn, who do I speak to about comps?
MISS THORN. I beg your pardon?
SYLVIA. Free tickets.
MISS THORN. I'm afraid the Turner School never gives away free tickets. The money, of course, will go to the school fund.
SYLVIA. I see. (*Under her breath as SHE goes.*) I'll bet the Lerman kid gets comps. (*SYLVIA exits, slamming the door.*)
JUDY. Thank you for coming, Miss Thorn.
MISS THORN. Please, call me Myrna. (*Pronounced Meeerna.*)
JUDY. You were an actress once ...
MISS THORN. (*Flattered.*) Why, yes, yes I was.
JUDY Was there ever a part you wanted that you didn't get?
MISS THORN. One or two. What's your point?
JUDY. I was hoping you could talk to Tina, as someone who's lived through similar disappointments. It might help her to put things in perspective.

(Music Cue 5B: BEFORE "THIRD GRADE" UNDERSCORE)

MISS THORN. I must admit, Mrs. Denmark, in all my years as a professional actress, and I've lived on both coasts ...
JUDY. My.
MISS THORN. ... I've never known anyone to want a part so desperately. It's as if starring in the school show means too much to Tina.
JUDY. That's what worries me.

(Music Cue 6: TEACHING THIRD GRADE)

MISS THORN.
THERE'S NO NEED TO WORRY
UNKNIT YOUR BROW
FOR THO' TINA'S TAKING THIS HARD RIGHT NOW
EXPERIENCE TELLS ME I'M HAPPY TO SAY
SHE'LL GET OVER HER DISAPPOINTMENT SOMEDAY.

She'll learn being a star isn't everything. There are many wonderful careers one can choose, that are equally rewarding and at least as exciting. Look at me!

TEACHING THIRD GRADE
SHAPING THE MINDS OF A NEW GENERATION
NO LONGER AFRAID
TO GET ON WITH MY LIFE AND OFF MEDICATION
SURE I WENT TO NEW YORK
TO BE AN OVERNIGHT SENSATION
MORE THAN A FACE
I WAS A WINNING COMBINATION
OF TALENT AND GRACE
I SHOULDA PACKED MACE
'CAUSE I WAS MUGGED, RAPED AND ROBBED
BEFORE I LEFT PENN STATION

NOW I'M BACK, LORD
AT THE BLACKBOARD
TEACHING THIRD GRADE
  JUDY. Miss Thorn ...
  MISS THORN. Eh ...!
  JUDY. Myrna ... don't you think it's a good idea for someone in show business to have something to fall back on?
  MISS THORN.
SOMETHING TO FALL BACK ON

SURE IT WORKS FOR SOME
BUT I FELL BACK
AND LOOK WHAT LIFE'S BECOME
TONIGHT I'LL GET COZY
POUR WINE, LIGHT THE TAPERS
THEN SIT THERE—ALONE THERE
ALL NIGHT GRADING PAPERS
THE PAY MAY BE STEADY
MY SUMMERS ARE FREE
BUT DO YOU WANT YOUR DAUGHTER
TO TURN OUT LIKE ME?

YEAH! I HAD SOMETHING TO FALL BACK ON
SAFE AND SO SECURE
WITH VERY FEW SURPRISES IN STORE
THIS CHEERY DEMEANOR
IT'S ALL A CHARADE
THE TRUTH IS I'M BORED
I HATE TEACHING THIRD GRADE
    JUDY. I wonder what's keeping Tina ...?
    MISS THORN.
SICK OF JANE AND SICK OF DICKY
NEVER QUIET—ALWAYS STICKY
    JUDY. Can I get you something?
    MISS THORN.
NOSES RUNNY! NOSES BLEEDY!
LITTLE RUNTS SO BLOODY NEEDY!
    JUDY. A Coke? A Triscuit?
    MISS THORN.
JOAN HITS JANICE WITH A SLINKY
BART MAKES TERRY TOUCH HIS WINKY
THIS ONE CRIED AND THAT ONE PEED
I CAN'T TAKE IT, GOD I NEED ...

(Looks around frantically and spots the liquor.)

SOMETHING TO FALL BACK ON ...

(Runs to the bar and pours a hefty drink.)

JUDY. Please, help yourself.
MISS THORN.
FROM WHAT I'VE FALLEN BACK ON ...
JUDY. About Tina ...?
MISS THORN.
AS FAR AS THE LEAD IN THE SHOW, MY DEAR
SHE'LL HAVE TO GET OVER
NOT WINNING THIS YEAR
INTO EACH LIFE RAIN FALLS I'M AFRAID
LIFE IS A BITCH ...
AND IT STARTS IN THIRD GRADE

(SHE drains her glass.)

JUDY. You couldn't make her a dream Pippi? Something like that?
MISS THORN. I'm afraid not.

(SYLVIA and TINA enter eating ice cream cones. SYLVIA has two scoops.)

SYLVIA. My dear Miss Thorn, have you considered letting Tina be the Lerman girl's understudy?
TINA. What's an understudy?
SYLVIA/MISS THORN. An understudy is ... *(THEY laugh and exchange glances.)* An understudy ...

(SYLVIA glares at THORN. THORN backs off.)

SYLVIA. ... is someone who plays the part if the star can't go on.
MISS THORN. We're only giving two performances, and I think having an understudy would be unnecessary. *(SYLVIA looks daggers at THORN.)* But, if it makes you all feel better, yes, Tina can be Louise Lerman's understudy.

TINA. Wait a minute. You expect me to learn all of Pippi's lines, and all of Pippi's songs, and there's a chance I won't get to play Pippi?
MISS THORN. That's correct.
SYLVIA. Unless, of course, something were to happen to Louise Lerman.

> (Music Cue 6A: SCENE 3 – PLAYOFF)

(SYLVIA smiles at TINA who thoughtfully licks her ice cream cone.)

TINA. *(Smiles.)* I'll do it!

(A flash of LIGHTNING and a crack of THUNDER. As the LIGHTS FADE, the eyes in Tina's portrait light up à la "Village of the Damned.")

BLACKOUT

SCENE 4:
THE DENMARK LIVING ROOM – THREE WEEKS LATER

JUDY and SYLVIA are finishing lunch at the kitchen table.

SYLVIA. That was a delicious lunch, dear. Thanks for inviting me.
JUDY. Well, you were still here from breakfast.
SYLVIA. Think those cookies are done?
JUDY. Now, Sylvia, they're for after the show tonight.
SYLVIA. Opening night. Oh, Judy, you must be so proud of Tina. I wish I had a daughter.
JUDY. But, I thought ...

SYLVIA. (*Sharply.*) A talented one!
JUDY. Would you like to talk about it?
SYLVIA. What is there to say? (Music Cue 7: WHERE TINA GETS IT FROM) But you would think that one's own flesh and blood would have inherited at least a fraction of her mother's talent.
JUDY. But who's to say where talent comes from. Look at Tina. Lord knows where she gets it from. After all ...
I CAN'T SING A NOTE
NO TALENT WHATSOEVER
I CAN'T TELL A JOKE
 SYLVIA. No?
 JUDY.
NO, I'M SIMPLY NOT THAT CLEVER
MAKE NO MISTAKE
WITH PRIDE I'M OVERCOME
BUT I HAVEN'T A CLUE
AS TO WHO
TINA GETS IT FROM
 SYLVIA. Surely there must be something even you can do.
 JUDY.
WELL ...
I CAN MAKE A BED
 SYLVIA. See, I told you.
 JUDY.
AND COOK A CHICKEN
 SYLVIA. You're brimming with talent.
 JUDY.
MY SMOKED SALMON SPREAD
 SYLVIA. Yummy!
 JUDY.
FRED SAID IS FINGER-LICKIN'
 SYLVIA. You must give me the recipe.
 JUDY.
BUT ON A STAGE
I SIMPLY WOULD GO NUMB

SO I'M UP IN THE AIR
AS TO WHERE
MY DAUGHTER GETS IT FROM
  SYLVIA.
SHE NEEDS SOMEONE LIKE ME, DEAR
I'VE BEEN AROUND THE BLOCK
AND TOGETHER WE'LL MAKE MILLIONS
SO WHO CARES WHERE TINA GETS IT FROM
NOW HERE'S THE WAY I SEE IT
FIRST WE GET AN AGENT
ONE IN NEW YORK, ONE ON THE COAST

SYLVIA.	**JUDY.**
SHE'S GREAT FOR COMMERCIALS	HEY …
BUT ONLY A COUPLE	I CAN COOK A CHICKEN
OVEREXPOSURE IS ALL TOO COMMON	MY SMOKED SALMON SPREAD …
IN THIS HIGHLY COMPETITIVE	
WORLD WHERE A PROFESSIONAL KID CAN MAKE MORE MONEY	FRED SAID …
THAN HER PARENTS	IS FINGER-LICKIN'
SHE NEEDS SOMEONE LIKE ME, DEAR	BUT ON A STAGE
I'VE BEEN AROUND THE BLOCK	I SIMPLY WOULD GO NUMB
AND TOGETHER WE'LL MAKE MILLIONS	SO I'M UP IN THE AIR
SO WHO CARES WHERE TINA GETS IT FROM	AS TO WHERE
	MY TINA GETS IT FROM

	NO MATTER WHERE SHE GOT IT
OH WHO CARES	
	SHE GOT AN AWFUL LOT
IT DOESN'T MATTER	MY KID'S A GENIUS
NOT A CRUMB	IT'S A MYSTERY TO ME
	I GUESS I'LL NEVER KNOW
WHERE TINA ...	WHERE TINA ...
GETS IT ...	GETS IT ...

(THEY dance.)

SYLVIA. Take me home!
JUDY. Where do you live?!

SYLVIA.	**JUDY.**
WHERE TINA	WHERE TINA
GETS IT FROM!	GETS IT FROM!

JUDY. I know one thing. Tina does not get her talent from me.
SYLVIA. What about Frederick?
JUDY. Who? Oh, my husband. He doesn't sing or dance at all ... I don't think.
SYLVIA. I've heard it said that talent often skips a generation.
JUDY. That may be true. I was adopted when I was very young.

(Music Cue 7A: SCENE 4 – UNDERSCORE)

SYLVIA. Were you ever curious about your real parents?
JUDY. Oh, no. I think the important thing is that I was raised by two wonderful people.
SYLVIA. Are they at all gifted?
JUDY. Dad ran a television network.

SYLVIA. No talent there.
JUDY. And Mother ... Mother positively hates anything to do with show business. She's a theater critic.
SYLVIA. Lita Encore!
JUDY. Have you heard of her?
SYLVIA. She's legendary. Your mother closed hundreds of shows. Thousands!
JUDY. She's coming to see Tina's show tonight.
SYLVIA. How exciting. I must ask her to autograph a copy of her book, "Ruthless: The Life and Times of Ruth DelMarco."
JUDY. (*Startled.*) That name!
SYLVIA. Ruth DelMarco?

(*JUDY jumps out of her chair.*)

SYLVIA. What's the matter, Judy?
JUDY. Didn't she...? Wasn't she...?
SYLVIA. She was an actress. Your mother wrote a book about her many years ago.
JUDY. I don't remember.
SYLVIA. She could have been the greatest entertainer of all time.
JUDY. What's become of her?
SYLVIA. Bad reviews. Bad bad. She's dead. It's all in your mother's book.
JUDY. Well, I feel sorry for her and everyone like her, because show people are doomed. Doomed to a lifestyle of booze, pills, and heavy meals late at night.
SYLVIA. Ahh, but that's show business.
JUDY. And that's what worries me, Sylvia, as far as Tina's concerned. That's not the life I want for my child.

(*A WHISTLE blows. JUDY takes the coffee cups to the kitchen. SYLVIA follows as LIGHTS FADE on the living room.*
Direct segue to Scene 5.)

SCENE 5: THE TURNER SCHOOL AUDITORIUM

MISS THORN drags in a piece of tropical scenery.

MISS THORN. Okay, let's take it from after the storm at sea. Now, I want all the children who drown in scene one to dry off and quickly change into your native costumes. Come on, people, work with me. This is a theater, not a playground. We are not here to have fun. Alright, here we go. Places. Go music.

(Music Cue 8: THE PIPPI SONG)

(LOUISE enters dressed as Pippi Longstocking.)

LOUISE. Coconuts! Mangoes! Grass huts! And, look, the Pago Pago Hilton! This must be Tahiti! And I'm Pippi! Pippi Longstocking. And now that you know who I am, I'd like you to meet my best friend. Careful you don't get fleas. My best friend's a dog. Come on, Puddles!

(A bored and unhappy TINA ambles on dressed as a poodle. SHE sulks in the background.)

LOUISE. (*Sings.*)
HOWDY DO
MY NAME IS PIPPI
P-I-P-P-Y

(THORN corrects her for the tenth time.)

MISS THORN.
I! P-I-P-P-I!
    LOUISE.
OH.

I NEVER BEEN TO SCHOOL—NOT ONCE
A FACT I CAN'T DENY
I NEVER LEARNED TO READ OR WRITE
I CAN'T SPELL HERMAPHRODITE
NEVER LEARNED ARITHMETIC
BUT I DON'T GIVE A LICK
   MISS THORN. Sing out, Louise!

(At this point, TINA begins to mark the Pippi number upstage of LOUISE.)

LOUISE.
IF YA NEVER BEEN TO SCHOOL
LIFE IS NOT SO GRIM
YOU NEVER HAVE HOMEWORK
AND YOU NEVER EVER HAVE TO TAKE GYM
I'M FREE AND HAPPY ALL DAY LONG

(Sensing movement behind her, LOUISE whips around, only to find TINA innocently posing as PUDDLES. LOUISE continues.)

LOUISE.
JUST SINGIN' AND DANCIN'
THE PIPPI SONG

(TINA continues to upstage LOUISE, as SHE mimes the following Pippi speech.)

   LOUISE. Puddles and I were in a terrible storm at sea. Our boat tipped over and everyone got killed. But Puddles saved my life and brought me to this tropical paradise. Way to go, Puddles! Shake!

(LOUISE extends her hand to TINA who just stares at her.)

   LOUISE. *(Whispers.)* You're supposed to shake my

hand.
TINA. Look, Louise, you're not the director.
LOUISE. But the script says we shake hands.
TINA. Yeah? Well I didn't get a script.
LOUISE. Miss Thorn ...!
MISS THORN. Tina, just give her your paw.
TINA. I just don't think Puddles would shake hands here, okay? Not after being shipwrecked and having to doggy-paddle fifty miles. I think Puddles would rather lie down.
LOUISE. I'm sorry, I can't act with this.
TINA. You can't act period.
LOUISE. Can too.
TINA. Prove it.
MISS THORN. Girls, please! Let's just take it from the Charleston.

(The GIRLS dance as the dialogue continues)

TINA. The only reason you got the part is because Mommy and Daddy bought it for you.
LOUISE. My parents may open doors for me, Tina Denmark, but I've got to back it up with talent.
TINA. Better get busy.
LOUISE. (*To THORN.*) Do I have to have a dog?
MISS THORN. Yes, Louise. Puddles saves your life.
TINA. Stupid.
LOUISE. Shiksa.
TINA. Amateur!
LOUISE. Chorus girl!
TINA. Miss Thorn, Louise called me a chorus girl!
MISS THORN. That's enough.
TINA. She's always calling me bad names.
LOUISE. Liar!
TINA. This morning she called me a stuck-up little bitch.
LOUISE. Did not!

TINA. Did too!
MISS THORN. Tina! Louise!
LOUISE. Bitch!
TINA. Asshole!

(SCHOOL BELL rings.)

MISS THORN. That's it! Tina, go to recess.
TINA. But Miss Thorn ...
MISS THORN. Now! *(TINA exits.)* Louise, take ten, and then I want to hear the Pippi ballad.
LOUISE. Is that the slow song?
MISS THORN. That's correct! *(Exiting.)* May I remind the cast we open tonight, and to be honest with you ... I wouldn't pay to see this!

(LOUISE starts to jump rope. TINA enters.)

TINA. If you let me play Pippi, I'll be your best friend.
LOUISE. Look, do you think I want to be in this stupid show? I think it's embarrassing. But it makes my parents happy, and when Mike and Betty are happy, I'm happy. Got it? Here. *(Hands TINA the jump rope.)* I gotta go practice my part.
TINA. But I've got to play Pippi!
LOUISE. You don't have the range! *(Laughs and exits.)*

(Music Cue 9: I ASKED POLITELY
& SCENE TRANSITION)

TINA.
I ASKED POLITELY
I SAID PLEASE

(SHE stares at the rope in her hands.)

NOW THERE'S NOTHING LEFT TO DO BUT ...

(TINA chases after LOUISE.)

BLACKOUT

(Direct segue into Scene 6.)

SCENE 6.
THE DENMARK LIVING ROOM –
AN HOUR LATER

SYLVIA enters from the kitchen glancing at her wrist.

SYLVIA. Oh dear, where's my watch?

(JUDY pokes her head in from kitchen.)

JUDY. You gave it to Tina. *(Ducks out.)*
SYLVIA. That's right. Anyway, I think it's time for the news.

(SYLVIA switches on the radio. The song is clearly familiar to her, a song from the past. SHE listens with tears in her eyes, swaying to the music.)

RADIO SINGER.
I'LL BE AN UNKIE'S MUNCKLE
I'LL BE A GUN OF A SON
EVERYTHING'S DUNKY HORY
WHEN YOU'RE MY BUNNY HUN
YEAH, YOU'RE THE WHITTEN'S KISKERS
AND I'M AN UNKIE'S MUNCKLE
AIN'T WE FOT GUN?
RADIO ANNOUNCER #1. That was vintage Ruth DelMarco singing "I'll Be an "Unkie's Munckle."

(SYLVIA quickly switches to another station as JUDY enters.)

ANNOUNCER #2. Time for the local news. It seems one of the students attending the Turner Elementary School accidentally hung herself with a jump rope after falling from a catwalk, high above the stage of the Vivian Vance Auditorium. School authorities are puzzled as to what the child was doing on the catwalk, since none of the children are union, therefore authorized to climb the dangerous walkway. The child's name is being withheld until the parents can be notified. Stay tuned to this station for more news, the weather, and the name of the dead girl. But first, here's something I know you'll enjoy—Miss Connie Francis. (*CONNIE sings "Who's Sorry Now?"*)[1]

JUDY. Sylvia!

(SYLVIA turns down radio.)

SYLVIA. It was not Tina. Tina is far too smart to go playing where she might get hurt, much less killed.

(PHONE rings.)

SYLVIA. You'll have other children, Judy. You're still young.

(Music Cue 9A: BEFORE "KISSES AND HUGS")

(JUDY answers in a panic. SYLVIA keeps an ear on the radio.)

---

[1]Permission to produce *Ruthless!* does *not* include permission to use this music. See Music Note on page ii.

RUTHLESS! 43

JUDY.
HELLO?
YES, THIS IS TINA'S MOTHER
I HEARD, MRS. WILSON ...!
   SYLVIA. There's more news about the accident.
   JUDY.
BYE!

(JUDY slams down the phone. SYLVIA turns up the volume.)

ANNOUNCER #2. The parents have been notified, so we are authorized to announce that the name of the dead child is ... Louise Lerman, daughter of Michael and Betty Lerman.

(JUDY breathes a sing of relief. SYLVIA's eyes light up.)

ANNOUNCER #2. Miss Lerman, who was to star tonight in her school production of "Pippi in Tahiti," would have been eleven years old ... tomorrow. Now back to Connie. (*More "Who's Sorry Now?"*)
   JUDY. That poor, poor little girl.

(SYLVIA switches off the radio, and digs through her purse.)

   SYLVIA. Poor Tina. She probably hasn't had a bite of lunch.
   JUDY. Oh, Sylvia, I don't know what to do.

(SYLVIA puts on her lipstick.)

   SYLVIA. Make her a sandwich.
   JUDY. I don't think she's ready for something like this.
   SYLVIA. We've still got eight hours. She'll be

ready!
JUDY. Good-bye, Sylvia.
SYLVIA. I'll be back.
JUDY. I know, Sylvia.

(SYLVIA flings open the front door. TINA enters. THEY exchange a look. SYLVIA dashes out.)

TINA. Hello, Mother.
JUDY. Hello, sweetheart.
TINA. Guess what? We missed lunch all because Louise Lerman got killed.
JUDY. Tina, would you like to talk about what happened to Louise?

(Music Cue 10: KISSES AND HUGS)

(TINA bursts into song.)

TINA.
I'M SO VERY LUCKY
THAT YOU ARE MY MOTHER
   JUDY. Sweetheart ...
   TINA.
YOU DON'T HAVE A SON
I DON'T HAVE A BROTHER
   JUDY. Darling ...
   TINA.
JUST ME, YOU AND DADDY
OUR OWN FAMILY
NO OTHER PARENTS COULD EVER BE
AS LOVING AS MY PARENTS ARE TO ME

(JUDY begins to cry.)

Why are you crying, Mother?
JUDY. That poor little girl. Tina ...

(JUDY pats her lap for TINA to sit.)

SOMETIMES THINGS HAPPEN
AS SAD AS CAN BE
  TINA.
CAN I HAVE A POPTART
AND GO WATCH TV?
  JUDY.
YOU'RE TAKING THIS TRAGEDY WELL
AND THAT'S GRAND
BUT IF YOU WANT TO CRY
OR HOLD MOMMY'S HAND
OR EVEN STOP SMILING
I'D UNDERSTAND

(TINA crosses away.)

  TINA. Why should I cry? I didn't get killed.

(JUDY, taken aback, starts for the kitchen.)

  JUDY. I'll get your poptart.
  TINA.
I THINK THAT MY MOMMY
COULD USE A FEW KISSES

(JUDY runs to TINA.)

  JUDY.
I'LL TRADE THEM FOR HUGS
  TOGETHER.
OH WHAT BLISS THIS IS

(TINA pecks JUDY's cheek and runs off to her bedroom. DOORBELL rings.)

  JUDY. I'll get it.

(JUDY opens the door. MISS THORN sweeps in dramatically, wearing dark glasses.)

MISS THORN. Hello, Mrs. Denmark. May I come in?
JUDY. Of course.
MISS THORN. Mind if I smoke?
JUDY. I don't have an ashtray. I'll get you a dish.
MISS THORN. Cigarette?
JUDY. No, thank you.
MISS THORN. Do you have one?
JUDY. I'm afraid I quit.
MISS THORN. Cold turkey?
JUDY. I don't think so, but I'll look. (*Exits to kitchen.*)
MISS THORN. I've just come from the Lerman's. Poor Betty. She just sat there, crying, and rerunning Louise's Burger King commercial over and over again.

(JUDY proudly returns with a turkey leg on a plate and sets it in front of MISS THORN.)

MISS THORN. Poor Louise. (*THORN spots the turkey and sobs.*) Please, forgive me. Lord knows I'm trying.
JUDY. We can all be at times.

(MISS THORN stares at JUDY.)

MISS THORN. Our school is presenting an assembly program in Louise's honor. The children are writing poems and preparing numbers from Broadway shows. I've worked up a little something myself.
JUDY. Sounds like a lot of fun. How much are tickets?
MISS THORN. Fifty bucks! The money will be used to purchase a memorial fruit and cheese basket for the Lerman family.

JUDY. How thoughtful. Fruit and cheese can be so comforting.
MISS THORN. Something sure smells good.
JUDY. I'm baking cookies. They were for after the show tonight, which, of course, has been canceled.
MISS THORN. Whatever gave you that idea?
JUDY. Well, I thought at least until ...
MISS THORN. I couldn't possibly disappoint all the other children. They worked so hard and are so eager to perform.
JUDY. Yes, but I think ...
MISS THORN. I think it's an excellent opportunity for the children to learn that the show must go on. By the way ... how's Tina?
JUDY. I hope you're not suggesting that Tina play Pippi tonight.
MISS THORN. She is the understudy.
JUDY. I know, but ...
MISS THORN. I've worked awfully hard on this production, Mrs. Denmark, and I think it's good. Maybe the best damn work I've ever done. (*Pulls a hefty script out of her bag.*) So that talented kid of yours better get busy and learn these lines.
JUDY. But it's wrong. Shockingly wrong. I won't allow it!
MISS THORN. Look, Mrs. D., (Music Cue 10A: MISS THORN THREAT – "THIRD GRADE" Reprise – JUDY DISCOVERS WIG) I've got enough problems with the Pippi people over the damn rights. They're not going to stop me and neither are you. Now, maybe I'll have to change the kid's name, but mark me well; Pippi, Schmippy, that kid of yours better be in costume, in make-up, and in place by 7:55, or I shall be forced to go to the police!
JUDY. The police?!
MISS THORN. I didn't want to have to bring this up, but it seems the Lerman kid's wig is missing.
JUDY. Why are you telling me this?

MISS THORN. Because, according to one of the other students, little Rachel Hobbs, Tina was seen chasing Louise, and snatching at her wig.

JUDY. My God, are you saying you suspect that Tina ...?

MISS THORN. I suspect nothing. Not a thing. The children were playing some sort of game, they got a little overexcited, and one of them got killed. No, I suspect nothing.

JUDY. Why don't you just come out and say it? I want you to look me straight in the eye and tell me that my eight-year-old child killed for a part in the school show?!?

MISS THORN. Not just any part, Mrs. Denmark. The lead! And she better be letter perfect by curtain time or I can promise you there will be an investigation!

(SHE thrusts the script at JUDY who reluctantly takes it. Tossing the Pippi costume in JUDY's lap, SHE sings:)

NOW I'VE ALTERED THE COSTUME
LOUISE WAS TOO BIG
OH, YOU'LL HAVE TO COME UP WITH
A RED BRAIDED WIG
SMILE, MRS. DENMARK
SHE'S GONNA BE GREAT

(Glances at her watch.)

GOOD GOD, IT'S TWELVE-THIRTY
AND THE SHOW STARTS AT EIGHT

(SHE hurries to the door and flings it open.)

Look on the bright side. Now you'll get comps! *(Exits.)*

(JUDY drops the script and costume on the coffee table

and takes the turkey plate to the kitchen. TINA peeks in from the hall. Seeing the coast is clear, SHE runs in, grabs the script and costume, and exits back to her bedroom. JUDY comes out of the kitchen, missing TINA by a split second. SHE looks around for the script and bag. Realizing that TINA must have taken them, SHE starts for the hall, passing TINA's schoolbag on the way. Suddenly SHE freezes, whirls around, eyes riveted on the schoolbag. Slowly, SHE picks it up, carries it to the sofa, unzips it, reaches in, and, trembling, removes Louise Lerman's Pippi wig.)

JUDY. (*Whispers.*) Tina!

(TINA bounds in.)

TINA. Did you call me, Mother?
JUDY. What are you doing with this wig?
TINA. What wig?
JUDY. Louise Lerman's Pippi wig.
TINA. Mother, can we have a ballet barre?
JUDY. Tina ...
TINA. Francine Gordon has a ballet barre her daddy made out of an old crutch.
JUDY. Don't change the subject. Now, how did you get this wig?
TINA. I found it after Louise had her ... accident.
JUDY. If that's true, Tina, why didn't you give the wig to Miss Thorn?

(TINA runs to JUDY and climbs into her lap.)

TINA. Because I was afraid. Afraid Miss Thorn would think I was naughty. I wasn't naughty, Mommy. I promise. (*SHE cries.*)
JUDY. Is this true, Tina, or are you acting?
TINA. It's all true, Mommy, please believe me. (*SHE buries her head in JUDY's neck and sobs ... a little too*

loud.)

JUDY. Oh, knock it off, Tina. (*SHE pins her to the sofa.*) You're not that good!

TINA. (*Coldly.*) What do you mean, Mother?

JUDY. You did it, didn't you?

TINA. You can't prove a thing! Not a thing!

JUDY. You killed Louise Lerman for a part in a play?!

TINA. Not just any part, Mother. The lead!

JUDY. I want to hear it. Start at the beginning and don't leave anything out.

TINA. Okay, Mother.

(*Sings:*)

HOWDY DO MY NAME IS PIPPI ...

JUDY. Not the play, Tina! Tell me what happened to Louise.

TINA. We got to rehearsal ...

JUDY. Go on.

TINA. We changed clothes ...

JUDY. Go on.

TINA. We did warm-ups ...

JUDY. Go on.

TINA. Louise hung herself ...

JUDY. Back up.

TINA. I told Louise how much I wanted to play Pippi. How important it was to me. She just laughed and said ...

(*TINA mouths the following.*)

LOUISE. (*V.O. with echo.*) You don't have the range! (*Laughs.*)

JUDY. Then what happened?

TINA. I chased her. I chased her up onto the catwalk. That's when she gave me the wig.

JUDY. Go on.

TINA. I asked her if that meant I could play Pippi and she said ...

(TINA mouths the following.)

LOUISE. *(V.O. with echo.)* Yeah, over my dead body!
TINA. So I wrapped her jump rope around her fat neck and pushed her over the side! *(Laughs maniacally.)*
JUDY. Oh, Tina, Tina!

(TINA breathes heavily, savoring the moment. SHE glares at the audience revealing her true ruthless nature. A moment later, SHE smiles her sunniest smile, her mask back in place.)

TINA. I wanted the part. What could I do?
JUDY. You could have hurt her, you didn't have to kill her.
TINA. I wasn't thinking. I was tired and I hadn't had my lunch.
JUDY. Tina, look at me, sweetheart. You've destroyed another life. You killed that little girl. Do you know what that means?
TINA. It means I'm playing Pippi!
JUDY. Go to your room! You're punished!
TINA. Why?
JUDY. You wouldn't understand.

(TINA picks up the wig.)

TINA. But, Mommy, the play ...!

(JUDY grabs the wig. THEY fight over it. JUDY wrestles the wig from TINA, and hands her the schoolbag.)

JUDY. Never mind the play. Just go to your room.

And don't you dare come out until I call you!

(*TINA exits. DOORBELL. JUDY runs around, not knowing what to do with the wig. SHE hides it under the sofa, and opens the door. SYLVIA, in a full-length fur, enters carrying a shopping bag.*)

SYLVIA. Is she ready? Is everything laid out? Make-up box, ballet shoes, her new opening night party dress ...
JUDY. What new opening night party dress?
SYLVIA. This one!

(*SYLVIA whips an unusually sophisticated leopard evening dress out of the bag.*)

JUDY. Honestly, Sylvia ...
SYLVIA. Oh, Judy, lighten up. (Music Cue 11: TALENT – Reprise) (*Hangs the dress up.*) It was on sale. I picked one up for myself.

(*SYLVIA whips open her fur coat. SHE is wearing an identical party dress. JUDY shrieks!*)

SYLVIA.
SHE'LL LOOK EVERY INCH A STAR
IN WHAT I BOUGHT HER
NOW IF SHE JUST REMEMBERS
ALL I TAUGHT HER
TONIGHT WILL LAUNCH HER NEW CAREER
IT WON'T BE LONG BEFORE THEY CHEER
THEY'LL GIVE US A STANDING OVATION, BRAVA!
I'LL MAKE THE KID A HOUSEHOLD NAME
WITH A TINA DOLL AND THE TINA GAME
SHE'S GOING TO BECOME A CORPORATION ...

(*SHE throws her head back and laughs. JUDY pounds*

her fists and stamps her feet.)

JUDY. Stop it, Sylvia!
SYLVIA. What's the matter, dear?
JUDY. I don't know how to say it.
SYLVIA. I know, you're grateful for everything I've done, but you needn't try to put it into words.
JUDY. That's not it.
SYLVIA. Oh.

(DOORBELL.)

JUDY. That must be Mother!
SYLVIA. Oh, God, she's not going to review the show tonight, is she?
JUDY. I hope not.

(Music Cue 12: I HATE MUSICALS)

(SYLVIA turns away. JUDY hangs up SYLVIA's fur and opens the door. LITA ENCORE bursts in, carrying a huge bouquet.)

LITA. Where's my granddaughter?
JUDY. I'm afraid she's being punished.
LITA. I must be in the wrong house. *(Laughs at her own joke and flings the bouquet at JUDY. Spots SYLVIA.)* Hello.
JUDY. Mother, this is Tina's manager, Sylvia St. Croix.

(SYLVIA whips around. The TWO WOMEN size each other up.)

LITA. Don't I know you from somewhere?
SYLVIA. I replaced Monica Breedlove in "Shirley, You Jest!"
LITA. Of course. *(Quoting her own review.)* "The

role of Shirley was taken over by an actress whose performance obviously peaked in the taxi on the way to the theater ..."

SYLVIA. That's me.

(LITA laughs.)

LITA. *(To JUDY.)* Now then, what's all this twaddle about my granddaughter being punished?
JUDY. I'm afraid that Tina ...

(TINA bursts in from the hall.)

TINA. Grandmother!
LITA. Darling! Have you been naughty?
TINA. Have you?
LITA. I love this kid.
TINA. How much?
LITA. This much! *(Arms extended.)*
TINA. More!
LITA. This much! *(Arms wider.)*
TINA. More!

(LITA grabs flowers from JUDY and flings them at TINA.)

LITA. *(Fed up.)* Oh, here.
TINA. Ooh! Look, Sylvia.
SYLVIA. Mine are in the car ... and they're bigger.
JUDY. Tina, I want you to go back to your room now.
SYLVIA/LITA/TINA. Aawwwwwwww!!
JUDY. You can visit with grandmother later.
TINA. Yes, Mother.
SYLVIA. Tina, darling, I think we better work on that Pippi ballad.
TINA. Yes, Sylvia.

RUTHLESS! 55

(TINA and SYLVIA exit.)

LITA. Now then, darling, let me look at you. You look ... *(JUDY stares at her.)* Anything wrong?
JUDY. Would you like a drink?
LITA. You going to have one?
JUDY. Probably.

(JUDY pours drinks.)

LITA. Now, tell Mother what's troubling you.
JUDY. Mother, you know that Frederick and I have always encouraged ...
LITA. Who?
JUDY. Frederick? My husband?
LITA. You're married?
JUDY. He's away so often. *(Crossing to LITA with drinks.)* Can't wait for you to meet him. *(THEY clink glasses.)* As I was saying, Freddy and I have always ...
LITA. Who?
JUDY. Freddy! It's short for Frederick!
LITA. Of course! Go on. Go on.

(LITA drains her glass.)

JUDY. We've always encouraged Tina to do whatever she wants, and as you know, all she's ever wanted was to perform.
LITA. She any good?
JUDY. But I don't want her to be a performer. I don't want her to ever set foot on a stage again. Ever! And that goes for tonight.
LITA. Darling, if you think I've driven all this way to sit through some f'chochta Pippi musical that does not star my granddaughter, you're out of your mind.
JUDY. But, Mother ...
LITA. Honey ...
IF I WANT TO SEE THEATRE

I GO SEE A PLAY
WITH NO SINGING AND DANCING
TO GET IN THE WAY
THEATRE IS LANGUAGE
AND THAT SHOULD BE ALL
MUSIC BELONGS AT THE CARNEGIE HALL

(SHE heads to the bar to refill her glass.)

NOT A REASON ON EARTH
AS FAR AS I KNOW
TO WRITE, MOUNT, AND OPEN A MUSICAL
  SHOW ...

    Honey, I've been a theater critic for a hundred years and it's always the same ...
THE STORY IS MOVING
CHOCK FULL OF SUSPENSE
THE PLOT TAKES A TWIST
AND THE MOOD IS INTENSE
THEN SOMEONE SINGS A SONG ...
LIKE THIS!
IT DOESN'T MAKE SENSE
PUH-LEEEZE ...
I HATE MUSICALS!

I HATE THE NEW SHOWS
THEY'RE NOTHING BUT SETS
I MISS THE VON TRAPP KIDS
THE SHARKS AND THE JETS
UNPLUG THOSE KEYBOARDS
GIVE ME REAL CLARINETS
MISS OTIS SAYS WITH NO REGRETS
I HATE MUSICALS

THERE DOESN'T SEEM TO BE A SHRED
OF ANYTHING NEW
THE HOTTEST SHOWS WERE ALL COMPOSED

BY LATE '62
NOW IF YOU WANT TO CREATE A SENSATION
USE A HOLLYWOOD STAR AND AMPLIFICATION!

AND WHETHER THE SHOW
IS A HIT OR A FLOP
THEY SELL T-SHIRTS AND CAPS
WITH THEIR LOGO ON TOP
SO EVEN THOUGH YOU HATE THE SHOW
AT LEAST YOU CAN SHOP
ONE SIZE FITS ALL
AT A MUSICAL!

I HATE THE GENRE
IT'S ALL SECOND RATE
WHEN FORCED TO SEE THIS DREK
I ALWAYS COME LATE
FROM OVERTURE TO CURTAIN CALL
IT ALL TURNS ME OFF
I SIT THERE AND COUGH
THE WHOLE NIGHT LONG
'CAUSE I HATE MUSICALS
BUT NOT AS MUCH AS
I HATE THIS SONG!

(On the applause, SHE crosses to the sofa. The moment SHE sits down, the MUSIC starts up, and SHE all too willingly takes center stage for an encore.)

HOW I HATED PHANTOM
DOWN TO EACH CANDELABRA
I TOOK THE BOOK ALONG
AND READ THROUGH LES MISERA-BLAH
WHEN IT COMES TO SUBTLETY
THE BRITS FALL A HAIR SHORT
IF I WANT HELICOPTERS
I'LL GO TO THE AIRPORT!

SO KEEP YOUR CHORUS LINES
OF GYPSIES AND MAMES
I'D RATHER SEE A FLICK
OR BOWL A FEW FRAMES

NO MATTER WHO IS STARRING
I'M NEVER ENTICED
IT'S WAY OVER-PRICED
AND I WON'T PAY
I HATE MUSICALS
BUT I FEAR THEY'RE HERE TO STAY
YES, I HATE MUSICALS
BUT NOT AS MUCH AS
I HATE BALLET!

(LITA sits on the sofa.)

JUDY. Much as I'd love to hear a third chorus, I've got to ask you something I've never asked you before. Who were my real parents?

(LITA is speechless. SYLVIA rushes in.)

SYLVIA. Tina's having her bath. Now then, Judy, about tonight. There's going to be a lot of photographers so be sure to wear something gorgeous. Maybe they'll do a mother-daughter spread.
JUDY. It's a school show, Sylvia.
SYLVIA. It's the start of her career.
JUDY. I'm not sure I want her to have such a career.
SYLVIA. What?
JUDY. You heard me.
SYLVIA. I'm not so sure you have a choice. Show business is in that child's blood.
JUDY. Don't say that. It's not true. It's not in my blood or in Frederick's.
SYLVIA/LITA. Who?
JUDY. Frederick! My husbaaaand!

SYLVIA/LITA. Oh.
SYLVIA. Please, Judy ...
JUDY. I've made up my mind. I want my child as far away from show business as possible.

(SYLVIA crosses away, distraught.)

LITA. What about what Tina wants?
JUDY. Tina will be happier in the Brownies.
SYLVIA. No! She'll die in the Brownies!! (Music Cue 12A: UNDERSCORE) *(Crossing to JUDY.)* Judy, how can you forget what it feels like when all the other parents crowd around and tell you how special she is, and what a wonderful mother you are for being so supportive.

(JUDY staggers away.)

SYLVIA. I think you do want this for Tina, but you're afraid. Afraid of how desperately you want it, and not just for Tina, but for yourself!
JUDY. That's not true, Sylvia.
SYLVIA. Admit it! Deep down it's you who wants to be a star!
JUDY. No!
LITA. Everyone does!
JUDY. Stop it!
SYLVIA. You're jealous of your own daughter's talent!
JUDY. I am deliriously happy leading my normal, ordinary life. And so too ... *(Sits defiantly.)* ... will my daughter!
SYLVIA. *(Mysteriously.)* "A normal life was not possible, nor is it for any poor creature driven by inherited talent." I'm quoting you Miss Encore. It's a passage from a book you wrote many, *many* years ago, "Ruthless: the Life and Times of Ruth DelMarco."
JUDY. That name!! *(Reacts uneasily.)*
LITA. Ruth DelMarco?

(JUDY shrieks.)

LITA. Ruth DelMarco was insane ... talented, somewhat, but totally insane. Imagine killing yourself over a bad review.
SYLVIA. A review written by Lita Encore.

(THEY face off.)

LITA. What of it?
SYLVIA. That show was to be Ruth Del Marco's comeback. A comeback after many long years of pain and recovery. She poured her heart and soul and every penny she had into that production, and your scathing review closed it after one lousy performance.
LITA. That's my job.
SYLVIA. If only you'd have been a little kinder, a little more encouraging with your review, Ruth DelMarco might still be alive.
LITA. *(Uneasy.)* Perhaps she is.
SYLVIA. What?
LITA. They never found her body. Just those big footprints in the sand and a suicide note.
SYLVIA. Surely you don't believe ...
LITA. Three years ago, Ruth DelMarco was spotted doing "I Do, I Do," in Bucks County.
SYLVIA. That's just a rumor.
LITA. Perhaps. But the fact is they never found her.
SYLVIA. Or her child.
JUDY. A child?
LITA. *(Quickly.)* Lunch almost ready, sweetheart?
JUDY. Ruth DelMarco had a child?
LITA. That's just another rumor. I'm starving.
SYLVIA. A little girl, I believe.

(TINA calls from offstage.)

TINA. Sylvia!
SYLVIA. Coming, Tina.

(SYLVIA crosses melodramatically to the hall. JUDY looks searchingly to LITA, who turns away, and stares uncomfortably out the window. Slowly, as if in a trance, JUDY wanders downstage.)

SYLVIA. She kept it quiet, of course. The child's father being the president and all.

(SYLVIA exits. JUDY collapses in the chair and stares at TINA's picture.)

LITA. *(Quietly.)* Judy?
JUDY. Oh, Mother, I want my child to be happy.
LITA. She is happy.
JUDY. I want her to be normal.
LITA. She is happy.
JUDY. Mother, who am I?
LITA. You're my daughter, and I love you very much.
JUDY. How much?
LITA. This much.

(SHE makes an "inch" and giggles. JUDY is mortified.)

LITA. Only kidding.
JUDY. Please, I've got to know! Who am I?
LITA. You're Judy.
JUDY. But where do I come from?
LITA. Sears! *(Laughs uncontrollably.)*
JUDY. You've got to tell me the truth! Who were my real parents?!
LITA. Please, Ginger ...
JUDY. Ginger?!
LITA. Err ... Uhh ... I mean Judy!
JUDY. You called me Ginger! *(SHE twitches.)*

LITA. I knew God would punish me for panning "Fiddler." Oh, sweetheart ... daughter. This is so difficult for me. For both of us. Come, we'll have a nice quiet lunch, just the two of us, and afterwards, a long, long talk. Please. We need time.
JUDY. Of course, Mother. I understand. (*Starts for the kitchen.*) I'll make lunch.
LITA. You're Ruth DelMarco's child!

(*JUDY staggers around the room.*)

JUDY. Oh my God! My God!
LITA. You tore it out of me!
JUDY. You mean to say I came from that ... that actress?!
LITA. I know what you're thinking and it's not true!
JUDY. I'm talented! God help me, I'm talented!
LITA. Darling, you're not. You never were. You've always been a tone-deaf klutz. Trust me.
JUDY. But it's there in my blood. The talent. The drive. The pathological need to be famous! God, I feel so cheap and dirty. How did this happen?
LITA. I heard Ruth had a child, and when she disappeared, I came looking ... and I found you. Alone, frightened, living in your mother's dressing room. Oh, Judy ...

(*JUDY rises like a phoenix.*)

JUDY. No! My name is Ginger DelMarco! (*Glamorous pose.*)

(*LITA sits JUDY in the chair and perches on the arm, comforting her.*)

LITA. You are my daughter, and I've raised you ever since you were two years old.
JUDY. Oh, Mother ...

LITA. Okay, seven, what's the difference? You've turned out beautifully. You can't sing or dance at all.
JUDY. How can you be sure?
LITA. You're married to a fine young man, Kenneth.
JUDY. Frederick!
LITA. And together you've given birth to ...

(TINA bursts in wearing the Pippi costume, minus the wig.)

TINA. *(Singing.)*
HOWDY DO
MY NAME IS PIPPI!
P-I-P-P-I

(TINA plops down on the sofa. JUDY stares at her.)

LITA. You must take care of your daughter.
JUDY. She ... she ...
LITA. She needs you.
JUDY. She ... she ...

(SYLVIA yells from offstage.)

SYLVIA. Tina, get back here!
LITA. She needs you now more than ever!

(JUDY sinks back in the chair, staring blankly into space.)

LITA. You know, I'm so glad we had this chance to talk. I feel so much better. I think I'll go freshen up. *(Grabs her purse.)* You might want to put a comb through your wig too, dear. Break a leg, Tina.
TINA. Thanks, Grandmother.

(LITA laughs and starts for the hall, almost colliding with SYLVIA. THEY slowly circle staring each other

down. SYLVIA hisses at LITA. Startled, LITA exits.)

SYLVIA. Alright, Tina, I want to see the Pippi ballad, from the top.
TINA. I'm tired, Sylvia.
SYLVIA. Come on, come on. It's almost there.

(Music Cue 12B: ANGEL MOM – 3 FALSE STARTS)

TINA. Okay, okay.

(JUDY's eyes follow TINA as SHE steps onto the coffee table and sings:)

TINA.
WHEN I WAS A LITTLE GIRL
A LITTLE GIRL OF SEVEN
MY MOMMY UNEXPECTEDLY
WENT ON A TRIP TO HEAVEN
AND DADDY DEAR ...
SYLVIA. No, Tina. It's too cute. In needs weight. Now, try it again.

(TINA sighs and begins again, singing with a dramatic edge.)

TINA.
WHEN I WAS A LITTLE GIRL
A LITTLE GIRL OF SEVEN
MY MOMMY ... *(Starts to cry.)*
SYLVIA. No tears, damn it! What did I teach you?
TINA. If I cry, the audience won't.
SYLVIA. Precisely. Now start again.
TINA. *(Quietly.)* No.
SYLVIA. Tina ...?

(TINA plops down on the sofa, defiantly.)

TINA. I'm tired and I'm hungry.
SYLVIA. You're a quitter.
TINA. It's a lousy song, anyway!
SYLVIA. There are no lousy songs. Just lazy singers. Here, I'll show you how it's done. (*SHE steps onto the coffee table and sings.*)

WHEN I WAS A LITTLE GIRL
A LITTLE GIRL OF SEVEN
MY MOMMY UNEXPECTEDLY
WENT ON A TRIP TO HEAVEN
AND DADDY DEAR ...
WOULD KISS MY TEAR
WHEN I WOULD START TO CRY ...
JUDY. (*Quietly.*) It's too big, Sylvia.

(*SYLVIA stops dead in her tracks. TINA looks curiously at her mother.*)

SYLVIA. I beg your pardon?
JUDY. It's too big. You want them to come to you.
SYLVIA. Well, excuse me, Judy, but what would you possibly know about it?

(*JUDY sits up in her chair.*)

JUDY. I know enough to see that you're pushing for results. (*SHE rises.*) You're not in the moment. (*SHE approaches SYLVIA.*) You're indicating!

(*SYLVIA "indicates" being crushed. TINA crosses to JUDY.*)

TINA. Mama, will you show me how it's done?

(Music Cue 13: ANGEL MOM)

(*TINA sits and watches attentively. A bewildered*

SYLVIA drifts upstage. Slowly, JUDY removes her apron, tosses it over her shoulder, and prepares to sing. SHE hesitates.)

JUDY. I can't.
SYLVIA. Yes, you can.
JUDY. *(Sings.)*
WHEN I WAS A LITTLE GIRL
A LITTLE GIRL OF SEVEN
MY MOMMY UNEXPECTEDLY
WENT ON A TRIP TO HEAVEN
AND DADDY DEAR ...
WOULD KISS MY TEAR
WHEN I WOULD START TO CRY ...
AND SAY THO' MOMMY'S DEAD
SHE'S OVERHEAD
AN ANGEL IN THE SKY

(SHE catches sight of her right hand as it gestures to the music. Her left arm involuntarily floats up from her side. SHE stares at her hands.)

Mama? M-M-Mama?

(SHE gains confidence and begins to use her arms.)

NOW WHEN I LAY ME DOWN TO SLEEP
I DON'T TURN OFF THE LIGHT
SO MOM CAN FIND ME WHEN SHE COMES
TO KISS MY CHEEK GOOD NIGHT
OF COURSE I RAISE MY WINDOW NOW
BEFORE I GET IN BED
I WOULDN'T WANT MY ANGEL MOM
TO BANG HER ANGEL HEAD

(SHE dramatically thrusts her right hand up to heaven.)

I'm a talented girl, Mama!

(THE transformation is complete. JUDY is show business personified as SHE belts out the rest of the number.)

JUDY.
YOU MAY SAY I'M MOTHERLESS
BUT I MUST DISAGREE
FOR I LIVE FOR MY MOTHER
AND MY MOTHER LIVES IN ME
AND EVERYTHING I'LL EVER DO
AND EVERYTHING I'LL BE
I'LL BE BECAUSE OF MOMMY DEAR
MY MOTHER LIVES IN ME!

Tina, take the third chorus!

TINA.
YOU MAY SAY I'M MOTHERLESS
BUT I MUST DISAGREE
   JUDY. *(Coaching.)* Arms!

(TINA uses her arms.)

TINA.
FOR I LIVE FOR MY MOTHER
AND MY MOTHER LIVES IN ME
   JUDY. Smile, baby!
TOGETHER.
AND EVERYTHING I'LL EVER DO
AND EVERYTHING I'LL BE
I'LL BE BECAUSE OF MOMMY DEAR
MOMMY'S HERE
MY MOTHER LIVES IN ME!

(Music Cue 13A: ANGEL MOM – PLAYOFF)

(JUDY bows to an imaginary audience. When TINA steps forward to join her, JUDY throws her arms open and whacks TINA in the head. At first stunned, and then horrified, TINA runs to SYLVIA, who stands watching JUDY with tears in her eyes. JUDY continues to bow. SHE grins at the audience as if to say ... "It's my turn.")

END OF ACT I

(Music Cue 14: ENTR'ACTE)

ACT II
PROLOGUE

The ACTORS are starkly lit representing various locations.

(Music Cue 15: ACT II – MONTAGE/OPENING)

JUDY.
SATURDAY THE TWENTY-THIRD OF MAY
FREDERICK, DARLING
WHAT CAN I SAY

Hello in person would be nice, but, I'm leaving you this note to tell you that our daughter has committed an unspeakable crime.

(LIGHTS UP on LITA reading a copy of "Variety.")

LITA. "The role of Pippi Longstocking was played by newcomer Tina Denmark. While possessed of a loud voice and a dazzling smile, I'm afraid Miss Denmark was more concerned with appearing cute, than with capturing the true essence of the complicated Miss Longstocking. Her performance was a tangle of childish posturing and cliché mannerisms. While this may be endearing at a playground, it simply does not belong on the stage. My money's on the electrifying Rachel Hobbs, who was utterly enchanting as Pippi's heroic dog, Puddles." (*SHE laughs.*)

(LIGHTS OUT on LITA.)

JUDY.
OH, WHAT'S TO BECOME
OF MY ONLY DAUGHTER
WHO I HAVE PROTECTED
FROM CROUP TO SPLIT ENDS
SO MANY LESSONS
THAT I SHOULD'VE TAUGHT HER
LIKE FOR EXAMPLE
TO NOT KILL HER FRIENDS

Our child needs the sort of help only a loving and courageous parent can provide. So I turned her in.

(LIGHTS UP on a veiled MISS THORN.)

PROSECUTOR. (*V.O.*) I call to the stand Miss Myrna Thorn. Tell us, Miss Thorn ...
MISS THORN. Eh—
PROSECUTOR. (*V.O.*) Myrna, in your own words, what you saw on the morning in question.
MISS THORN. She pushed her. Wham! Bam! Right off the catwalk. She's the devil's spawn! (*Lifts her veil and smiles.*) Are we on TV?

(LIGHTS FADE on MISS THORN.)

JUDY. Perhaps my biggest mistake was letting Sylvia handle her defense.

(LIGHTS UP on SYLVIA addressing the "Jury.")

SYLVIA. Ladies and gentlemen of the jury, let us concentrate on the real issue here, shall we? The fact is the Lerman girl was horribly miscast, therefore, I tell you, justice has been served!

(We hear a judge's GAVEL banging. LIGHTS UP on all awaiting the verdict.)

JUDGE. (*V.O.*) Order. Order in the court. Tina Denmark ... I hereby sentence you to the Daisy Clover School for Psychopathic Ingenues.

(*ALL gasp as a cell door slams. LIGHTS FADE on ALL except JUDY.*)

JUDY. As for me, now that I know the truth about myself—who I am, what I've got burning inside of me—there's nothing left to say but, by the time you read this, I will be gone. (*Exits.*)

(*LIGHTS UP on SYLVIA.*)

SYLVIA. Judy Denmark was gone alright. Gone off in search of her true identity, leaving behind her only daughter, locked away in a reform school for the criminally talented.

(*A LIGHT comes UP on TINA at the Daisy Clover School for Psychopathic Ingenues. SHE scrubs the floor on her hands and knees.*)

TINA.
I AM AT THE DAISY CLOVER SCHOOL
AN ACTRESS PAYING DUES
JUST ONE OF SEVERAL HUNDRED
PSYCHOPATHIC INGENUES

(*As TINA reads a telegram, we hear JUDY's voice.*)

JUDY. (*V.O.*) Greetings from New York City. Stop. Sorry I can't make it to Parent's Day. Stop. Gotta run. Opening on Broadway ... mine! Wish me luck! Mother.

(*TINA crumples up the telegram and scrubs.*)

TINA.
THE OLDER GIRLS ARE DANGEROUS
THEIR SMOKING MAKES ME COUGH
MY LIFE IS TAKING ORDERS
WHILE MY MOTHER'S TAKING OFF!

ANNOUNCER. (*V.O.*) This year's Tony Award goes to Ginger DelMarco for "Entres Gnu."

(A burst of applause. A RAT scurries by TINA.)

TINA.
I MUST CONFESS
IT REALLY MAKES ME BURN
A MOTHER SHOULDN'T TAKE
HER DAUGHTER'S TURN

(TINA storms off stage. SYLVIA appears and addresses the audience.)

SYLVIA. Talent! Inherited and unstoppable, dragging generation after generation into the spotlight. Meet Judy Denmark, who now, just two years and two Tony Awards later, is known only by the name her biological mother gave her ...

(End of PROLOGUE. Direct segue into ACT II, Scene 1.)

ACT II:
GINGER DELMARCO'S PENTHOUSE APARTMENT IN NEW YORK CITY

The CURTAIN parts as GINGER DELMARCO sweeps downstage.

SYLVIA. ... Ginger DelMarco! Ginger DelMarco, a born again talent who hasn't baked a cookie in years.

(GINGER laughs. The PHONE rings. SHE ignores it.)

SYLVIA. A star package bursting with agents, *(PHONE rings.)* lawyers, hair dressers, and ...

(EVE enters from the terrace.)

EVE. I'll get it.

(PHONE rings.)

SYLVIA. ... her devoted personal assistant ... Eve.

(EVE answers the phone.)

EVE. DelMarco residence.
SYLVIA. Eve ... a clutching, clawing Broadway wannabe, clinging oh, so desperately to the hem of success.
EVE. I'm sorry, Miss DelMarco never comes to the phone. You'll have to wait until she calls you.

(EVE holds the phone out to GINGER.)

GINGER. Bye-bye!

(EVE slams down the phone. GINGER roars with laughter and starts offstage, EVE imitating her every sound and move.)

SYLVIA. As for Tina ...

(GINGER exits. EVE holds back and eavesdrops on SYLVIA.)

SYLVIA. I have her last letter here. It has obviously been censored. *(Reading a letter that has bits cut out.)* "Dear Sylvia, I am writing to ... the ... that ... are ... whenever ... please ... if possible. Tina" On the very morning that Tina was to be released, I had the continental breakfast at Lindy's and headed straight to Ginger's apartment. *(Exits.)*

(Music Cue 16: PENTHOUSE APARTMENT)

EVE.
THAT'S PENTHOUSE APARTMENT
A VIEW OF THE PARK, OH
LIFE IS A LARK, OH
FOR GINGER DELMAR-CO
THE LIVIN' IS EASY
FROM MORNING TO NIGHT, OH
YOU KNOW YOU'RE A STAR
WHEN YOUR TABLE LIGHTERS LIGHT, OH!

HEY LOOK AT ME, OH
A KID FROM TOLEDO
LIVIN' THE HIGH LIFE
I WISH IT WERE MY LIFE
BEIN' PERSISTENT
I BECAME HER ASSISTANT
I SOAK UP HER GLAMOUR
AND SOMETIMES I AM HER

I PUT ON HER UNDIES
HER PERFUME AND JEWELS
I SLIP INTO HER NIGHTGOWN
AND SLAP ON HER MULES
I GUZZLE HER LIQUOR
I EAT ALL HER FOOD
I CUDDLE HER TONY'S
WHEN I'M IN THE MOOD

I SPRAWL ON HER BED
I READ ALL HER MAIL
I STUDY HER MOVEMENTS
EVERY DETAIL
I WANNA BE READY
FOR ONE DAY PERHAPS
I'LL BE WAITIN' IN THE WINGS
WHEN GINGER SNAPS!

I PICK UP HER TISSUES
WHEN SHE HAS THE FLU, CHOO
I PUMICE HER BUNIONS
THIS WEEK SHE HAD TWO, EEW
I COOK AND CLEAN
I WASH AND SEW
I WALK THE DOG
AND SHOVEL SNOW
I'M A GLORIFIED ... MAID!
BUT I'M HAVIN' THE TIME OF *HER* LIFE
AND GETTIN' PAID

(SHE straightens up the apartment a bit, then falls to her knees desperately.)

I WANT A PENTHOUSE APARTMENT
A VIEW OF THE PARK, OH YEAH!

(DOORBELL.)

EVE. I'll get it. (*SHE picks up the phone.*) DelMarco residence, hello? Hello???

(*DOORBELL. Realizing it's the doorbell, SHE hangs up and crosses to the door and opens it. SYLVIA barges in carrying the Pippi wig.*)

SYLVIA. Hello, Eve.
EVE. Hello, Miss St. Croix. How did you get past the doorman?
SYLVIA. Easy. I didn't wake him up. Is she here?
EVE. Yes, but you know Miss DelMarco never receives visitors. You'll have to wait until she calls on you. Bye-bye.

(*SYLVIA removes her fur and hurls it at EVE, who in turn hurls it off the balcony.*)

SYLVIA. This is the thanks I get for everything I've done for her. Now that she's a star she's turning her back on her past. (*Crosses to the bar, drops the wig, and mixes a drink.*) She thinks she doesn't need me. (*Yelling.*) Well, I don't need you, Miss Broadway star!

(*PHONE rings.*)

EVE. I'll get it. (*Runs to the phone.*)
SYLVIA. Miss "I-don't-need-anyone-for-anything!"

(*EVE answers the phone.*)

EVE. DelMarco residence.
SYLVIA. Miss "I-did-it-all-by-myself!"
EVE. You may send her up. (*Hangs up.*)
SYLVIA. Miss "Thanks-a-lot-and-out-with-the-garbage!"
EVE. I'm afraid it's time for Miss DelMarco's

interview. The reporter is on her way up. Maybe you'd better leave.
SYLVIA. Is she afraid I'll talk ... tell the world she has a family?
EVE. That's impossible. Miss DelMarco has no family, she's dedicated to her career.
SYLVIA. Not to mention a daughter in a reform school! I'll wait.
EVE. Can you wait by the elevators?
SYLVIA. I will wait right here, thank you very much.
EVE. Suit yourself. I'll get it!

(DOORBELL. SHE makes a face and runs to the door and opens it. EMILY BLOCK enters and brusquely offers her hand.)

MISS BLOCK. Emily Block, "Modern Thespian."
EVE. Hiya, Miss Block. Can I take your coat?

(SHE retracts her hand suspiciously.)

MISS BLOCK. Are you the maid?
EVE. I'm Miss DelMarco's personal assistant. Name's Eve.

(THEY shake.)

MISS BLOCK. You can never be too careful in New York City.
EVE. *(Whispers.)* I'm an actress too, you know. Want to take my picture?

(MISS BLOCK pins her against the door.)

MISS BLOCK. *(Flirting.)* Maybe later. *(To SYLVIA.)* Hello. Emily Block, "Modern Thespian."
SYLVIA. Yes, I'll bet you are.

MISS BLOCK. I am as the good Lord made me.
SYLVIA. Taxi!
EVE. Miss St. Croix was just leaving, weren't you, Sylvia?
SYLVIA. My card. (*Hands BLOCK a card.*)
MISS BLOCK. Sylvia St. Croix. Are we French?
EVE. Hah!
SYLVIA. St. Croix is a stage name. My real name is ...

(*GINGER sweeps into the room carrying a fancy party dress. SHE finishes Sylvia's sentence:*)

GINGER. "... Sylvia St. Sydney. Need I say more?" Here! (*Flings the dress at EVE.*) I got a stain on this.
EVE. Yes, Miss DelMarco.
GINGER. I told you to speak French!
EVE. Oui, Miss DelMarco. (*Curtsies.*)
SYLVIA. We ... have to talk.
GINGER. Call my press agent. (*Spots MISS BLOCK.*) Who the hell are you?
MISS BLOCK. Emily Block, "Modern Thespian." (*Extends her hand.*)
GINGER. (*Whispers.*) That's entirely your affair. (*To EVE.*) The heave-ho.
EVE. C'est publicite.
GINGER. (*Sweetly.*) Hello. Sylvia, Eve, give us a few?
EVE. Come on, Sylvia, you can help me spray for roaches. (*Crossing behind GINGER, SHE hisses:*) Don't scratch your scabs or they'll never get any better!
GINGER. (*To BLOCK.*) She's nuts but I don't pay her much.
EVE. Sylvia! (*Exits.*)

(*Reluctantly, SYLVIA rises.*)

GINGER. (*To BLOCK.*) Please, make yourself at

home.

(SYLVIA and BLOCK sit.)

SYLVIA/BLOCK. Thank you.
GINGER. *(To SYLVIA.)* Not you!

(SYLVIA exits in a huff.)

MISS BLOCK. And what a lovely home it is.
GINGER. Thanks.
MISS BLOCK. Tell me, do you prefer living in the city as opposed to, let's say, the suburbs?

(Music Cue 16A: UNDERSCORE)

GINGER. Oh, I'm a city girl through and through. Always have been, always will be.
MISS BLOCK. I see.
GINGER. I just seem to thrive on the hustle and bustle. Sure I'd love a little more space, who wouldn't, but just look at the view.

(GINGER flings open the terrace door. We hear CAR HORNS, SIRENS, SHOUTING, GUNSHOTS, SCREAMS. SHE closes the door.)

MISS BLOCK. You're immensely successful.
GINGER. You peeked.
MISS BLOCK. But, tell me, does it bother you when a critic writes, and I quote, "Ginger DelMarco is not a real actress. Just a no-account entertainer wasting her life doing musicals."
GINGER. *(Chiming in with her.)* "... no-account entertainer wasting her life doing musicals." That's just Mother being a bore.
MISS BLOCK. That's right, your mother's a critic.
GINGER. Everyone's a critic!

MISS BLOCK. Were you close with your natural mother, the fabulous Ruth DelMarco?

(Music Cue 16B: UNDERSCORE)

GINGER. Mother and I were inseparable. (*Noticing BLOCK not writing, SHE repeats herself pointedly.*) Mother and I were inseparable! (*BLOCK writes.*) I used to live in her dressing room. Her costumes were my friends, her props, my toys.
MISS BLOCK. I was a great fan of your mother's.
GINGER. Let's talk about me!
MISS BLOCK. Two years ago you were an overnight sensation.
GINGER. Overnight! That's rich. You work a lifetime perfecting your technique ... voice lessons, acting classes, years of dance. (*Thrusts out her leg.*) Look at that line!
MISS BLOCK. Where'd ya study?
GINGER. Europe!
MISS BLOCK. Now you're the toast of Broadway.
GINGER. You're too kind.
MISS BLOCK. Or should I say Danish?

(GINGER rises.)

GINGER. Danish?
MISS BLOCK. Didn't it used to be Denmark?
GINGER. Denmark?
MISS BLOCK. As in Judy Denmark?
GINGER. Don't be ridiculous.
MISS BLOCK. As in two years ago you were a house-wife!
GINGER. (*Calling offstage.*) Guards! (*To BLOCK.*) Who are you? What do you want? You want Eve? You can have Eve! (*Calling.*) Eve!
MISS BLOCK. I want an exclusive. The Judy Denmark story. Your story.

GINGER. I don't give exclusives.
MISS BLOCK. Look, honey, this house-wife thing's gonna break wide open whether you like it or not. I'm giving you the chance to tell it in your own words.
GINGER. Can I sing it?
MISS BLOCK. Please.
GINGER. (*To MUSICIANS.*) Boys?

(Music Cue 17: IT CAN NEVER BE THAT WAY AGAIN)

(Intro starts.)

ONCE LIFE WAS SIMPLE
AND ENTRES NOUS
I WAS AN ORDINARY NOTHING
JUST LIKE YOU ...

Sorry.

OH HOW I LOVED TO COOK AND CLEAN
MY LIFE AN OPEN MAGAZINE
JUST LIKE EVERY HAPPY HOUSEWIFE
WAY BACK WHEN
IT CAN NEVER BE THAT WAY AGAIN

I LOST THE APRON
AND FOUND MY VOICE
NOW I LIVE MY LIFE ON STAGE
I HAVE NO CHOICE
A WOMAN DOOMED TO ENTERTAIN
MUST USE APPLAUSE TO EASE THE PAIN
WHEN SHE GETS THAT OLD FAMILIAR
HOUSEWIFE YEN
BUT IT CAN NEVER BE THAT WAY AGAIN.

Do you think I like this? Do you think I want this? I was happy and fulfilled as a housewife. Now look at me.

You think I wouldn't give up a sold-out matinee to do a couple loads of laundry? Do you know what it's like to lie there in bed, night after night, fighting an urge to defrost your freezer? Or to iron? Just a pillowcase. A hanky. But I can't. I can't. I'm a star!

NOW PEOPLE LOVE ME
FROM HELL TO MAINE
SO IT'S GOOD-BYE TO APPLE PIE
BON JOUR CHAMPAGNE
PERHAPS TO YOU THIS WON'T MAKE SENSE
I'LL ALWAYS MISS MY PICKET FENCE
AND THE WAY MY LIFE WAS SIMPLE
WAY BACK WHEN
BUT NOW I STAR IN BROADWAY SHOWS
'CAUSE IN MY VEINS THE TALENT FLOWS

This time I'm doing it for me, Mama!

IT WILL NEVER BE THAT WAY AGAIN
MISS BLOCK. And now, Miss DelMarco, I'd like to hear more about ...

(GINGER spots the Pippi wig and screams.)

GINGER. Auugghh! (Music Cue 17A: UNDERSCORE) What the hell is this doing here?

(SYLVIA enters from the kitchen.)

SYLVIA. I thought it might remind you.
GINGER. I can't imagine of what.
SYLVIA. Don't you know what day it is?
GINGER. Tuesday?
SYLVIA. Tuesday, October the sixth.
GINGER. My God! My nail wrap!
SYLVIA. Today's the day your daughter is being released!

MISS BLOCK. You have a daughter?
GINGER. (*Quickly.*) Would you like to see the rest of the apartment?
MISS BLOCK. Where is she?
GINGER. Eve!
MISS BLOCK. Is she as talented as her mother?

(*EVE enters from the kitchen.*)

EVE. Oui, Miss DelMarco?
GINGER. Show Miss Block around.

(*GINGER tosses the wig to EVE as SHE passes. EVE ushers MISS BLOCK to the kitchen.*)

EVE. C'mon, c'mon, let's go, let's go. Everybody stay together.

(*EMILY casually touches something. EVE swats her with the Pippi wig.*)

EVE. Don't touch anything! We are now entering the kitchen ...
GINGER. While you're in there, fix me a snack!
EVE. Oui, Miss DelMarco.
GINGER. Pancakes Barbara!

(*THEY exit.*)

SYLVIA. I don't trust that girl.
GINGER. She makes good pancakes.
SYLVIA. Speaking of which, you're putting on weight.
GINGER. And you're my manager, not my mother.

(*Tension mounts as SYLVIA and GINGER face off. GINGER yells offstage to the pianist who's been playing underscoring.*)

GINGER. Knock it off! (*MUSIC abruptly stops.*) Sylvia, it's not that I don't appreciate everything you've done for me, but look at me, darling, I've outgrown you.
SYLVIA. I made you a Broadway star!
GINGER. Of musical comedy. Damn it, Sylvia, I want to act! Incidentally, I'm leaving for the coast tomorrow to do a screen test.
SYLVIA. Movies! I should've known. Well, you can't leave. You have a show to do and your understudy broke her neck.
GINGER. She started it.
SYLVIA. I can't believe you're giving up the stage.
GINGER. That's really none of your bee's wax.
SYLVIA. All of your bee's wax is my bee's wax.
GINGER. Not any more.
SYLVIA. What are you saying?
GINGER. I want out of out our contract.
SYLVIA. You can't mean that.
GINGER. I'll give you anything you want. A new car. An acting school for kids. A Mary Kay franchise. Anything.
SYLVIA. But you need me!
GINGER. Do I?
SYLVIA. Ginger …!
GINGER. Let me go, Sylvia.
SYLVIA. I can't.
GINGER. You've got to let me go!

(*SYLVIA turns away dramatically.*)

SYLVIA. Very well. You'll give me anything I want?
GINGER. Name it.
SYLVIA. I want Tina.
GINGER. Oh, Tina, Tina, Tina, Tina.
SYLVIA. She's finished her term at Clover. Arrangements must be made.
GINGER. What sort of arrangements?

SYLVIA. Clearly you have no time for her. You have no time for anyone but yourself. What that child needs ...
GINGER. I know what she needs, Sylvia, I'm her mother.

(SHE takes a piece of candy from a dish, goes to eat it, decides not to, puts it back.)

GINGER. And if you think for one second I will allow my child to be in show business ...
SYLVIA. You signed a contract.
GINGER. I don't care.

(Over Sylvia's next speech, GINGER goes for the candy, and again, fighting temptation, puts it back.)

SYLVIA. Look, I know how you used to feel about Tina and show business, but, surely, all of that has changed now that you're a star yourself.
GINGER. Exactly! Now that I'm a star, I know this rotten business inside out, and I do not want any child of mine anywhere near it. *(SHE gobbles the candy.)*
SYLVIA. Afraid of the competition?
GINGER. Butt out, Sylvia!

(Music Cue 17B: I WANT THE GIRL)

(GINGER storms off.)

SYLVIA.
YOU SAY THAT I CAN HAVE ANYTHING
THAT I WANT
I WANT THE GIRL
YOU SAY THAT YOU WILL PAY ANY PRICE
MAY I BE BLUNT?
I WANT THE GIRL
LOOK AROUND
LOOK WHAT I MADE HERE

I DIDN'T DO IT FOR YOU
I'M NOT CUTTIN' OUT TILL I'M PAID, DEAR
SO SAVE YOUR BEHAVIOR
IT'S MUCH TOO ABUSIVE
I WANT THE GIRL
AND I WANT AN EXCLUSIVE

YOU THINK THAT YOU CAN TEAR US APART
YOU'VE GOT YOUR NERVE
I'LL GET THE GIRL
SO HOPELESSLY WRAPPED UP IN YOUR LIFE
YOU DON'T DESERVE
THAT LITTLE GIRL
TRUE, YOUR REVIEWS MAY BE GLOWING
THE CRITIC'S DARLING THEY SAY
WELL DARLING YOUR EGO IS SHOWING
TODAY'S HOT TAMALE
TOMORROW GROWS COLDER
THE FUTURE IS HERE DEAR
LOOK OVER YOUR SHOULDER

I'M GONNA TAKE HER
AND I'M GONNA MAKE HER
A BIGGER STAR
A BRIGHTER STAR THAN YOU

I CAN'T LET IT HAPPEN
NOT AGAIN
I CAN'T FACE THE LOSS
NOT AGAIN

PICKING OUT A DRESS
WORKING ON YOUR SMILE
REMEMBERING YOUR LINES
FORGETTING YOU'VE A CHILD
LADY YOU'RE ON TOP
GO ON AND TAKE A BOW
GO ON AND TAKE ANOTHER

HOW CAN YOU BE BLAMED
YOU'RE NO DIFFERENT FROM YOUR MOTHER

STAND BACK
THIS TIME SHE'S HITTIN' THE HEIGHTS
THAT GORGEOUS FACE
THOSE GOLDEN CURLS
I SEE A BLAZING THEATRE MARQUEE
MY NAME IN LIGHTS
I MEAN THE GIRL'S

ONE DAY YOU MAY UNDERSTAND DEAR
MAYBE YOU'LL THANK ME SOME DAY
FOR TAKING THESE MATTERS IN HAND, DEAR
NOW GO ON AND POLISH YOUR STAR AS IT RISES
BUT DON'T BURN YOUR BRIDGES
LIFE'S FULL OF SURPRISES

I'M GONNA TAKE HER
AND I'M GONNA MAKE HER
A BIGGER STAR
A BRIGHTER STAR THAN YOU
JUST WAIT AND SEE
I WANT THE GIRL
I'LL GET THE GIRL
I WANT THE GIRL
TO BE ME
TO BE ME
BE ME!
BE ME!
TO BE ME!

(EVE and MISS BLOCK ENTER.)

EVE. And that concludes our tour. Don't forget to sign the mailing list. Anybody want a drink?

(GINGER storms on.)

GINGER. Yes!

(EVE pours GINGER a drink, chugs it, pours another.)

SYLVIA. You must excuse Miss DelMarco. She's a trifle on edge. You see, today is the day her daughter ...
GINGER. No need to apologize for me, Sylvia. *(Sits next to MISS BLOCK.)* Please, forgive me.
MISS BLOCK. Perfectly alright. I can be a real bitch myself sometimes.

(GINGER touches EMILY'S knee.)

GINGER. I like you.

(EMILY smiles. GINGER pulls her hand back.)

GINGER. As a friend! Eve, crush me an aspirin.
EVE. Oui, Miss DelMarco.

(EVE hands GINGER the drink and runs off.)

GINGER. Sylvia, care to freshen up?
SYLVIA. Thank you, dear, I don't mind if I do.

(SYLVIA starts for the stairway.)

GINGER. I meant in the lobby!

(THEY face off.)

SYLVIA. I'm not leaving until we've got a deal. *(Starts for powder room.)*
GINGER. Yeah? Well, try not to get make-up all over my hand towels.

(THEY hiss and spit at each other. SYLVIA storms off. GINGER glares at MISS BLOCK who is seated on the sofa, feverishly taking notes.)

GINGER. Sit down, you're making me nervous!

(A confused EMILY glances around, stands then sits. The PHONE rings. GINGER ignores it. After the third ring, EVE staggers in half undressed with a bottle of scotch and a smoke.)

EVE. Can somebody get that? *(Exits.)*

(GINGER glares at EMILY who answers the phone.)

MISS BLOCK. Hello? *(Pronounced "Yellow.")* Uh huh ... uh huh ... uh huh ... *(Laughs.)* It's for you. *(Hands GINGER the phone.)*
GINGER. Thanks. *(Takes phone.)* Yeah? *(Under.)* I see. Thank you. *(Hangs up.)* I hope you got everything you wanted.
MISS BLOCK. Well, no, actually, I had a few more questions I'd like to ask you.

(GINGER hustles MISS BLOCK to the door.)

GINGER. And your questions are so interesting ... so provocative. So sorry I can't offer you anything. It's not that I don't love to entertain ... I just don't! Bye-bye!

(Music Cue 17C: U.S. GINGER OPENS DOOR)

(GINGER opens the door to usher MISS BLOCK out. TINA stands pathetically in the doorway, wearing a tattered full-length sweater, and holding a battered suitcase. Her hair has been chopped off. Wordlessly, TINA enters and crosses to the sofa, taking in the room. GINGER whispers to MISS BLOCK:)

GINGER. One of the neighbor's kids. I baby sit to earn a few extra bucks. (*Pushing MISS BLOCK out the door.*) Be a doll and don't put that in the article.
MISS BLOCK. How about a picture?
GINGER. Why not? (*SHE poses dramatically.*)
MISS BLOCK. Not you, the kid!
GINGER. Get out! (*Slams the door in her face, then dramatically:*) Hello, Tina.
TINA. Hello, Mother.
GINGER. You look different.
TINA. So do you.
GINGER. You look beautiful.
TINA. So do you.
GINGER. You look older.
TINA. So do ...
GINGER. (*Quickly.*) Please, sit down. (*Calling offstage.*) Eve, where's my aspirin?

(*TINA sits ladylike on the sofa. EVE enters wearing the dress Ginger handed her earlier.*)

EVE. I'm sorry, Miss DelMarco, I can't find the aspirin. (*Spots TINA.*) How 'bout a Valium? (*Plops down next to TINA.*) Hello.
TINA. How do you do?
GINGER. Tina, how would you like to see Mommy on Broadway tonight?
TINA. I don't have any money.
GINGER. Don't be silly, sweetheart, I get free tickets.

(*EVE jumps up.*)

GINGER. Ticket! I get one free ticket!

(*EVE plops down.*)

EVE. Say, aren't you the dame who killed that little girl for a part in a play?
GINGER. Not just any part ... the lead!
EVE. How'd ya do it?
GINGER. She threw her off a catwalk. (*Laughs.*)
TINA. That was a long time ago.
GINGER. Certainly was. Remember that? God, I was so angry at you. Now there are a few actresses I'd like to throw off a catwalk.
EVE. Me too! (*Laughs.*)
GINGER. That'll be all, Eve. Go polish my Tony.
EVE. Which one?
GINGER. (*Coos.*) I love it when you ask me that. (*Snaps.*) Both of them! And take off my dress.

(EVE crosses to GINGER and begins to unzip her.)

GINGER. The one you're wearing!
EVE. But I thought you gave it to me.
GINGER. To take to the cleaners, Einstein, not to wear.
EVE. Whoops!
GINGER. Oh, and Eve...?
EVE. Oui, Miss DelMarco?
GINGER. You're fired!
EVE. You can't fire me because I quit! (Music Cue 17D: UNDERSCORE) I hate you. I've always hated you. You and your phony ways. Speaking lousy French and reading book reviews like they was books. It's Ginger this, Ginger that. It's all about Ginger. Well, when is it all about Eve?

(Chasing EVE off stage.)

GINGER. Pack your bags and get out!!
EVE. Can I keep the dress?
GINGER. Get out!

(EVE runs off. There is an uncomfortable silence.)

GINGER. I'm sorry, I haven't been to visit you more often. At school, I mean.
TINA. That's okay. I had a ton of homework.
GINGER. I hope you got the birthday money.
TINA. Yes, thank you.
GINGER. Did you buy something pretty-pretty?
TINA. Oh, no. I gave it all to charity. It made me feel good. In here. *(Points to heart.)* Tell me, Mommy, how do you feel? *(Points to hear.)* In here.

(Uncomfortable pause, then:)

GINGER. Hey, did you know that "Pippi in Tahiti" made it to Broadway?
TINA. I hear you were very good.

(Music Cue 17E: UNDERSCORE)

GINGER. Well, it's a good part. They say I can play anything, you know?
TINA. Can you play the part of my mother again? I want to go home. I want to go back to the way it was when we were a family.
GINGER. You don't understand. That's impossible. We just can't go back there, and that's all.
TINA. But why? Why?
GINGER. For one thing, I've sold all the furniture.
TINA. I can make some. I've had two years of woodshop.
GINGER. Sit down, Tina, I've got something to show you. *(Gets a book and reads.)* "Ruthless: The Life and Times of Ruth DelMarco. Talent! Where does it come from? Is it a product of environment? Or is talent something you're born with. Something in the blood." *(Closes book.)* I know the answer now. Ruth DelMarco was my mother.

TINA. Are you saying that show business is in my blood?
GINGER. It's too late for me, but you, you're still young and strong. I want you to fight it!
TINA. But, Mommy ...
GINGER. It's not Mommy anymore! It's Mommy ... darling! And as your mother, it's my duty to protect you from this evil business, that takes and takes and takes and takes and takes and takes and gives so little in return.
TINA. But, Mommy ...!
GINGER. Go now!
TINA. The truth is, I don't want to be in show business. Not anymore. It was a hard couple of years but I learned something. I learned that wanting to be rich and famous is an empty ambition. It's what's in your heart that really counts. I know, the applause is wonderful, but you can't take the audience home with you after the show.
GINGER. Well, not all of them anyway.
TINA. But your fans can't hold your hand when you're afraid, or tuck you in and kiss you goodnight. No, nothing can take the place of loved ones. Of family. Let me stay. I can make you happy again.
GINGER. Oh, Tina, there is something missing from my life.
TINA. I know.
GINGER. Do you?
TINA. I brought you a present. (*TINA opens her suitcase.*)
GINGER. A present? Pour moi? Quelle surprise! I just love presents! What is it? No, don't tell me. (*Covers her eyes.*) Let me guess.

(*TINA places something wrapped in tissue paper on GINGER'S lap.*)

TINA. I made it myself.
GINGER. Something in wood? (*Laughs.*)

TINA. Open it.

(GINGER tears open the package and takes out an apron.)

TINA. Put it on, Mother.

(GINGER stares at TINA.)

GINGER. I don't think so.
TINA. But it's your only chance to save yourself.
GINGER. Tina ...
TINA. Don't you see, I came back because you need me. We must take care of each other now. Please don't send me away.

(TINA cries softly. GINGER goes to comfort her, but as GINGER strokes her hair, TINA over does it, and we hear the same fake crying from ACT I.)

GINGER. Oh, knock it off, Tina. You're not that good. You never were. What are you really doing here?

(Music Cue 17F: UNDERSCORE)

(TINA drops the act and rips off her sweater revealing a starlet outfit underneath. SHE slaps on a glittery cap. SHE is hard as nails.)

TINA. What do you think I'm doing here?
GINGER. How the hell should I know? I'm a Broadway star, not a Broadway mind reader.
TINA. I want what I've always wanted.
GINGER. And what, pray tell, is that?
TINA. To be the star in this family.
GINGER. How dare you!
TINA. You owe me this.
GINGER. Come again?

TINA. You turned me in, just when I could've had a career.
GINGER. Let's not get nuts, Tina, it was a school show. Besides, I did it for your own good.
TINA. Bullshit! You did it for your own good. All so you'd be free to run to New York and have my career. Well it won't wash. I'm back! And you're my mother, so you better start acting like it!

(Music Cue 18: PARENTS AND CHILDREN)

(TINA thrusts the apron at GINGER who throws it down.)

GINGER.
YOU'RE NOT MY ONLY REASON TO EXIST, DEAR
WHEN I THINK OF ALL THE LIFE
I MIGHT HAVE MISSED, DEAR
YES, I HAD A LIFE BEFORE YOUR BIRTH, DEAR
YOU'RE NOT MY ONLY REASON TO BE LIVING
HERE ON EARTH, DEAR

BEING A MOTHER
IS ONLY A FRACTION
EVEN A MOTHER'S
ENTITLED TO ACTION
DON'T GET ME WRONG, KID
I KNOW THE SCORE
BUT I'VE DONE DOUBLE DUTY
AND NOW I WANT MORE

I FED YOU
I DRESSED YOU
YOU SNEEZED
AND I GOD BLESSED YOU
NOW I HAVE A LIFE
I'M MORE THAN A MOTHER
I'M MORE THAN A WIFE

TINA.
I AM YOUR KID AND
THERE'S NO GOING BACK, MOM
I'M HERE AND NOW
I THINK I'LL GO UNPACK, MOM
WHATEVER I AM, MOM
I OWE IT TO YOU
SO YOU CAN'T DISREGARD ME
AND DISCARD ME ON CUE
MY LAWYERS ALL AGREE
GOOD OR BAD LUCK, MOM
YOU'RE STUCK, MOM
WITH ME
  GINGER.
LET'S BE CALM
LET'S NOT SHOUT
LET'S TRY AND UNDERSTAND
WHAT THIS IS REALLY ALL ABOUT
  BOTH.
WHO'D HAVE THOUGHT WE'D COME
TO THIS POSITION
MOTHER DAUGHTER LOCKED IN COMPETITION
  GINGER.
AND ALL I'M WANTING
  TINA.
ALL I'M SAYING
  GINGER.
ALL I'M HOPING
  BOTH.
ALL I'M PRAYING
IS FOR YOU TO LOOK AT ...
  TINA.
ME
  GINGER.
LOOK AT ME
  TINA.
LOOK AT ME

GINGER.
LOOK AT ME
   TINA.
LOOK AT ME
   GINGER.
ME!
   TINA.
ME!
   GINGER.
ME!
   TINA.
ME!
   BOTH.
LOOK AT ME!

PARENTS AND CHILDREN
SO OFTEN LIKE STRANGERS
COMPETE FOR ATTENTION
VIE FOR RESPECT
PARENTS AND CHILDREN
ACTING LIKE STRANGERS
AND IF YOU TAKE A MOMENT
TO REFLECT
YOU'LL SEE
WE'RE NO DIFFERENT
FROM ANY FAMILY
   TINA.
YOU'RE MY MOTHER
   GINGER.
YOU'RE MY DAUGHTER
   BOTH.
LOOK AT ME!
   TINA. How could you?
   GINGER. Excuse me?
   TINA. How could you leave your only child?
   GINGER. The same way my mother left me!

(SYLVIA enters.)

SYLVIA. Something she has regretted every minute of her life. (*Dramatically.*) Hello, Tina.
GINGER. All my mother cared about was her career. Can't say that I blame her.
SYLVIA. Your mother is so very proud of you.
GINGER. My mother's dead.
SYLVIA. Am I? (Music Cue 18A: UNDERSCORE) The critics tried to kill me, but I'm still here.
GINGER. I don't understand, Sylvia.
SYLVIA. No, my child. Not Sylvia. The name's DelMarco! (*Whips off her wig to reveal long blond hair.*) Ruth DelMarco!
GINGER. M ... m ... Mama? M ... m ... m ... Mama?
SYLVIA. Yes, Gingie ... Mama! After Lita's poisonous review closed my show I couldn't face anyone. Not even my own child. Then, when they canceled my booking on the Joe Franklin show, I knew it was over for good. I swam far, far out to sea, but as luck would have it, I was rescued by a passing cruise ship. Fortunately, no one recognized me with wet hair. One night I sang a couple of songs in the Lido Lounge, and realized I had to perform again. Soon I was headlining ... and calling bingo, in the main room. Or I should say Sylvia St. Croix was. They loved me!
TINA. They'll love anything on a cruise ship.

(SYLVIA glares at TINA.)

SYLVIA. Then one day a producer came aboard and offered me a part in an all-white company of the all-black version of *Hello Dolly*. I jumped at it. Years later I played your small town, and that's when I spotted you. All those years how I hoped and prayed that my little Gingie might take a lesson, develop a glimmering of talent. But suddenly, it didn't matter. For there standing next to you was my granddaughter ... Tina. Tina had it all, the looks,

the drive, the talent, and I knew God was giving me a second chance. (*Pause.*) Can you ever forgive a silly, selfish, old woman?
GINGER. You're not silly. (*SYLVIA reacts.*) But why didn't you tell me all this before?
SYLVIA. I didn't want you to think I was hanging around trying to get a part in one of your shows because I was your mother, or anything. (*No response from GINGER.*) Even a smallish part. (*Still no response.*) I've got my pride.
GINGER. Pride is a luxury a woman on stage can't afford. What I can't understand is why did you try to take Tina from me?

(*SYLVIA turns away.*)

SYLVIA. I was thinking of another little girl. A child kept hidden away in her mother's dressing room. I couldn't let you make the same mistake with your daughter. You'd never forgive yourself.

(*GINGER holds out her hand.*)

GINGER. I forgive you, Mama.
SYLVIA. Gingie ...?
GINGER. Hold me, Mommy!
SYLVIA. Baby!

(*SYLVIA runs to GINGER. THEY embrace.*)

GINGER. My hair! My hair!
TINA. Grandmother!
SYLVIA. Granddaughter!

(*THEY all embrace.*)

GINGER. You know what? You are going to be in my new show!

SYLVIA. That's very generous of you, darling, but the truth is, I don't want to perform anymore. What I really want to do is direct.
GINGER. Then you'll direct it.
TINA. Hey, what about me?
SYLVIA. She'd be great in the part of your daughter.
GINGER. Sorry to disappoint you, but the part's been cast.
SYLVIA. Oh, dear.
TINA. Does she need an understudy?

(GINGER and SYLVIA throw back their heads and laugh.)

TINA. I want that part.
GINGER. You're not ready for it. I know you're good, but are you tough enough? Sure, you got rid of the competition once, but do you know how many people you have to destroy if you're ever going to make it in this business?
TINA. I can learn. Teach me?

(GINGER steps forward to sing. So does TINA and SYLVIA. GINGER glares at them and THEY quickly move upstage. Just as GINGER opens her mouth to sing, EVE enters carrying a suitcase.)

(Music Cue 19: RUTHLESS)

EVE. Well, I guess this is good-bye.
GINGER. Not now, Eve.
EVE. I just wanted to say ...
GINGER. I'm singing, Eve.

(EVE exits in a huff.)

GINGER.
I REMEMBER THE NIGHT

WHEN I WON MY FIRST TONY
I THANKED MY PRODUCERS
THE GANG DOWN AT SONY
I THANKED MY DIRECTOR
MY HAIRDRESSER, PAUL
I THANKED ALL THE PEOPLE
BOTH LITTLE AND SMALL
AND I ASSURE YOU THE TEARS THAT I DABBED
WERE NOT FOR THE BACKS THAT I STABBED

BE ... RUTHLESS
TAKE A GANDER AT ME ... RUTHLESS
UNCONDITIONALLY ... RUTHLESS
THAT'S THE GAME YOU MUST PLAY
TO HIT THE HEIGHTS
   SYLVIA.
I GUARANTEE ... RUTHLESS
PUTS YOU ON THE MARQUEE ... RUTHLESS
THEY'RE NOTORIOUSLY ... RUTHLESS
   SYLVIA/GINGER.
THOSE WHO HAVE A CAREER, DEAR-Y
   TINA.
BEING SWEET AND AFFECTIONATE
ONLY LEADS TO REJECTION, IT
NEVER WINS YOU A TONY AWARD
   GINGER.
LORD, YOU'VE HELPED ME
FIND MY NICHE
THANKS TO TALENT I'M FILTHY RICH
   SYLVIA.
THO' GOD KNOWS
YOU'RE A RUTHLESS BITCH
   GINGER. Thanks, Mom!
I'M FLYING HIGH AND ADORED!
   ALL THREE.
WE ... RUTHLESS!
   TINA.
GRANNY, MOMMY AND ME

ALL THREE.
RUTHLESS!
TAKE A TIP FROM THE THREE RUTHLESS
LADIES SINGING THIS SONG
CAN THE COMPASSION
THE FASHION IS RUTHLESS
  GINGER. *(To TINA.)*
WHETHER YOU'RE YOUNG
  TINA. *(To SYLVIA.)*
OR YOU'RE GRAY-HAIRED AND TOOTHLESS
  ALL THREE.
THE KEY TO SUCCESS
IS RUTHLESSNESS!
  GINGER.
A LOW-CUT DRESS
MIGHT IMPRESS
BUT TO GET THE GIG
YOU GOTTA HAVE BIG
RUTHLESSNESS!
  ALL THREE.
THE KEY TO SUCCESS
IS RUTHLESSNESS!
  TINA. Hey, let's all pile in a limo and go to Sardi's.
  GINGER. Hey, let's not and say we did. Besides, I got a show to do.

(EVE saunters on, a carbon copy of GINGER. Same hair, same clothes, same jewelry.)

  EVE. You just run along and have a good time, and don't you worry about the show. I can do it!
  GINGER. Over my dead body.

(EVE whips out a gun and points it at GINGER.)

  EVE. Suit yourself.

  (Music Cue 20: UNDERSCORE END OF SHOW)

GINGER. Eve!
EVE. No! The names not Eve! The name's ... Lerman. Betty Lerman!
GINGER/TINA /SYLVIA. Who???
EVE. Louise's mother ... Act One!

(EVERYONE gasps.)

EVE. I've waited a long time for this.
SYLVIA. I told you to check her references.
TINA. *(Distracting her.)* Hey, Betty, how's the lumber game?

(The moment EVE is distracted, GINGER rushes her.)

GINGER. Give me that gun!

(THEY struggle, moving in a circle.)

EVE. Bitch!
GINGER. Bitch!
EVE. Bitch!
GINGER. Bitch

(GUNSHOT. THEY step apart and uniformly check themselves for bullet holes. EVE raises her hand.)

EVE. It's me. *(Stumbles to the couch, dropping the gun on the coffee table.)*
GINGER. Don't get blood on my sofa!
EVE. Yes, Miss DelMarco.
GINGER. French?
EVE. Oui, Miss DelMarc ... ohh! *(SHE dies.)*
GINGER. Tina, you saved my life.

(TINA grabs the gun and aims it at GINGER.)

TINA. Now can I be in your show?
SYLVIA. No, Tina, not this way.
TINA. Back off, Sylvia, I've killed before.
GINGER. You wouldn't hurt Mommy, would you?
TINA. Oh, so it's back to Mommy, is it?

(LITA bursts in carrying a large bouquet of flowers.)

LITA. Where's my granddaughter?

(SYLVIA rushes TINA. THEY struggle for the gun.)

SYLVIA. Give me the gun, Tina. Careful, baby, that's the trigger.

(GUNSHOT. THEY step apart and uniformly check themselves for bullet holes. SYLVIA raises her hand.)

SYLVIA. It's me. *(Stumbles to the sofa.)*
LITA. Why, Ruth DelMarco. You're not dead!
SYLVIA. Give me a minute, Encore. *(Collapses.)* Come here, Tina.
TINA. I don't want to get blood on my outfit.
SYLVIA. Tina, I'm dying ...
TINA. You're dying?
SYLVIA. I'm afraid so.
TINA. Who's gonna handle me?
SYLVIA. C.A.A.! All the way! Remember, Tina ...

(As SHE sings SHE waves the gun wildly causing EVERYONE to duck.)

YOU CAN GO FIRST CLASS
IF YOU'VE GOT TALENT
THE WORLD WILL KISS YOUR ASS
IF YOU'VE GOT TALENT
BABY, YOU'VE GOT IT ALL, DON'T YOU SEE
AND ALL OF THAT TALENT CAME

FROM ... MMM ... MMM ... MMM ...

(SHE "dies.")

LITA. Ahh, she never could sing.

(LITA laughs. SYLVIA pops up, plugs LITA, and dies. LITA collapses on the sofa ... dead. GINGER picks up the apron and wanders in a fog.)

GINGER. What happened? Where am I? Who am I?
TINA. You're Ginger DelMarco.

(GINGER stares at the apron.)

GINGER. No, my name is Judy. (*Slowly puts on the apron.*) Judy Denmark. Judy Denmark, that's my name. Judy. Judy Denmark.
TINA. Judy?
JUDY. Please, call me Mommy.
TINA. Mommy?
JUDY. Tina?
TINA. Mommy!

(THEY run to each other and embrace.)

TINA. Mommy!

(As THEY embrace JUDY glances at the dead bodies.)

JUDY. I think we've learned a lesson here, Tina. Now together we can break the chain and once and for all give up show business. We'll lead a normal, ordinary life. Get your suitcase, sweetheart, we're going home! (*TINA runs for her suitcase.*) Because, as God is my witness, neither I nor my child will ever set foot on a stage again. Who needs Broadway?
TINA. You're right, Mother. (*Points the gun at her.*)

There's no money on Broadway. (*Plugs JUDY.*) I'm gettin' a series!

(*TINA grabs her suitcase and sings:*)

YOU CAN CALL THE SHOTS
IF YOU'VE GOT TALENT
THE WORLD IS GONNA PLOTZ
FROM ALL THIS TALENT
AND WHY BE IN A BROADWAY SHOW
WHEN YOU CAN STAR ON VIDEO
AND NOT HAVE TO LIVE IN THIS SLUM
HEY HOLLYWOOD ... HERE I COME!

(*SHE shoots the gun in the air, and storms out the front door. A moment later, a MAN carrying a briefcase enters.*)

FREDERICK. Honey, I'm home!

(*Final CURTAIN*)

(MUSIC CUE 21: BOWS)

(*CURTAIN CALL*)

THE COMPANY.
HE ... RUTHLESS
UNDENIABLY
SHE ... RUTHLESS
EVERYBODY'S A WEE RUTHLESS
SOMEWHERE DEEP IN THEIR HEART
SO IF YOU'RE SMART YOU'LL ...
CAN THE COMPASSION
THE FASHION IS RUTHLESS
WHETHER YOU'RE YOUNG
OR YOU'RE GRAY-HAIRED AND TOOTHLESS
THE KEY TO SUCCESS
IS RUTHLESSNESS!

(After final curtain as audience exits: Music Cue [pre-recorded])

<u>UNKIE'S</u> <u>MUNCLE</u>

I'LL BE AN UNKIE'S MUNCLE.
I'LL BE A GUN-OF-A-SON
EVERYTHING'S DUNKY-HORY
WHEN YOU'RE MY BUNNY-HUN

WELL IT JUST SHOWS TO GO YA
THAT THE RIME IS TIGHT
FOR YE AND MOO TO UDDLE CUP
AND NANCE, NANCE, NANCE ALL DIGHT

MORE THAN A BITTLE LIT I LOVE YOU
AND I'LL BE SHIPPED IN DIT YOU LOVE ME TOO
LALA-HOOYA

I'LL BE AN UNKIE'S MUNCLE
I'LL BE A GUN-OF-A-SON
EVERYTHING'S DUNKY HORY
WHEN YOU'RE MY BUNNY-HUN
YEAH YOU'RE THE WHITTEN'S KISKERS
AND I'M AN UNKIE'S MUNCLE
AIN'T WE FOT GUN?

COSTUME LIST

The costumes should be colorful and playful. Act I should have a distinct "fifties" feel, Act II should reflect the early "sixties."

JUDY DENMARK
A perky, pastel house dress worn with a tie-back apron.
A full-length bathrobe underdresssed with a glamorous and flowing lounging attire. (Ginger)

SYLVIA ST. CROIX
Smart, theatrical clothing. Auntie Mamish. Fur coats, jewelry. An outrageous, gaudy party dress that must be duplicated in Tina's size (Used as a prop only.)

TINA DENMARK
A bright and bouncy little girl dress with lots of petticoats.
Tap shoes in Scene 1.
A tacky, homemade poodle costume.
A replica of Louise's Pippi costume
A long, dowdy sweater-coat that is ripped off to reveal a dazzling "star outfit."

LITA ENCORE
Stylish suits with Hedda Hopper-type hats.

MYRNA THORN
School marm. Sweater over the shoulders. Sensible shoes.
Black hat w/veil (~~Prologue~~) Montage.

LOUISE
Plain-jane school dress.
Homemade, tropical Pippi costume complete with Pippi wig.

EVE
Secretarial skirt and blouse.
Elaborate cocktail dress.
Tan raincoat and hat.

(Identical Dress to Ginger)

EMILY BLOCK
Fashion victim. A vision in yellow. Suit with padded shoulders and short skirt. Big cap with black and yellow checkerboard brim. Black Georgie boots.

FREDERICK
Business suit with tie that matches Judy's house dress.

PROPERTY PLOT

ACT I

Scene 1: (preset)
Portrait of Tina with light-up eyes (back wall)
Framed photo of Tina (on phone table)
Can of Pledge and dust rag (under bar)
Decanter with liquor (bar)
Four glasses (bar)
Table radio (bar)

(personal)
Breakfast tray (Judy)
  w/ coffeepot
  coffee cup
  toast on a plate
Business car (Sylvia's purse)
Paper money (Sylvia's purse)
Wristwatch (Sylvia)
Gaudy ring (Sylvia)

Scene 2:
8 x 10 picture w/resume on back (Tina)
Cricket clicker (Miss Thorn)
Large stack of 8 x 10 pictures (Miss Thorn)

Scene 3:
Ice-cream cone, one scoop (Tina)
Ice-cream cone, two scoops (Sylvia)

Scene 4:
2 coffee cups (kitchen table)
Coffee pot (kitchen)

Scene 5:
Pages from "Pippi In Tahiti" script
Jump rope (Louise)

Scene 6:
Lipstick (Sylvia's purse)
School bag w/Pippi wig inside (Tina)
Handkerchief (Thorn)
Turkey leg on plate (kitchen)
Shopping bag (Thorn)
   w/full "Pippi" script, very thick
   Pippi costume
Shopping bag (Sylvia)
w/Tina's party dress on hanger
Large bouquet of flowers (Lita)

ACT II

Prologue:
Copy of *Variety* (Lita)
Bucket and sponge (Tina)
Folded letter (Tina)
Folded telegram (Tina)
Scurrying rat

Scene 1: (preset)
Working table lighter (coffee table)
Liquor (bar)
Cocktail shaker (bar)
Glasses (bar)
Crystal candy dish w/candy (bar)
Copy of "Ruthless: The Life and Times of Ruth DelMarco" (behind bar)

(personal)
Letter w/bits cut out (Sylvia)
Pippi wig (Sylvia)
Shoulder bag (Block)
   w/note pad and pencil
Business card (Sylvia)
Cocktail dress later worn by Eve (Ginger)

Half empty bottle of scotch (Eve)
Lit cigarette (Eve)
Small suitcase w/ "Clover" on it (Tina)
 gift-wrapped homemade apron inside
Large suitcase (Eve)
Hand gun (Eve)
Very large bouquet of flowers (Lita)
Briefcase (Frederick)

RUTHLESS!

SET and LIGHTING DESCRIPTION
ACT I

The Denmark Home

A perfect home. A cheery, colorful, almost dollhouse-like environment, consisting of a central living area with a stairway (or hallway) to offstage bedrooms, a swinging door which leads to an offstage kitchen, a front door, and perhaps a bay window which allows you to see characters approaching the front door.

Furnishings are comfy and reflect the mid-fifties: a three-seat sofa, coffee table, armchair, end table (w/telephone), a small dining table (w/two chairs), and a console table to hold the radio and liquor set-up. Many pictures of Tina at various ages decorate the walls, including a large portrait upstage center (see lighting). A backdrop may be used to establish middle-town America.

The Turner School Auditorium

Both scenes at the school, as well as the ACT II Montage, are played in front of a curtain hanging downstage of the basic set. The show curtain may be used as long as there is at least six feet playing space from the edge of the stage.

ACT II

Ginger DelMarco's New York Penthouse Apartment

A glamorous, glitzy Broadway star's pad complete with a sliding door to a small terrace, huge windows, a curved staircase leading offstage to the second floor bedrooms, and a front door that when opened reads "P.H.B."

Furnishings are arty and contemporary: a three-seat sofa and coffee table, a side chair and table, a mod cocktail bar w/two stools, over which hangs a gaudy chandelier. Pictures and show posters featuring Ginger DelMarco are everywhere. A dramatic New York skyline serves as a backdrop.

LIGHTING

Though this is not a traditional musical with chorus numbers, the lights should be colorful and bright with spotlights when possible.

Special Notes:

Sylvia's opening lines are played in a single spot in front of the curtain, which opens (or bleeds through if using a scrim, then opens) to reveal the fully-lit Denmark home.

The portrait of Tina should be rigged so that the eyes light up red on cue. An eerie up-light should be placed under Tina for her confession of the crime.

The ACT II montage should be done on a dark stage using specials to light each character as they speak. A prison bar template should be used on Tina.

Chaser lights for the "Ruthless!" number and curtain call a plus!

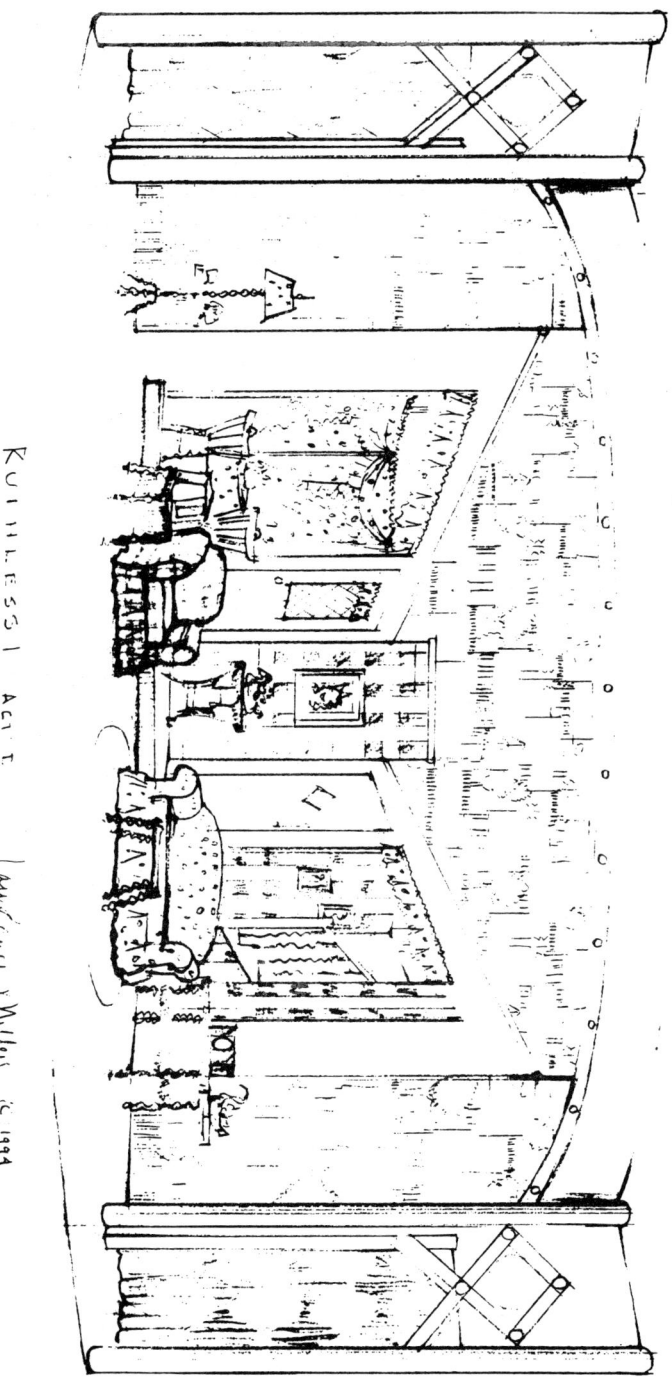

RUTHLESS! Act I Lawrence Miller © 1994

These RUTHLESS! scenic designs are for informational purposes only.
License to produce RUTHLESS! does not include permission to use these designs in conjunction with your production.

Ruthless! Set Designs © 1994 Lawrence Miller. All rights reserved.

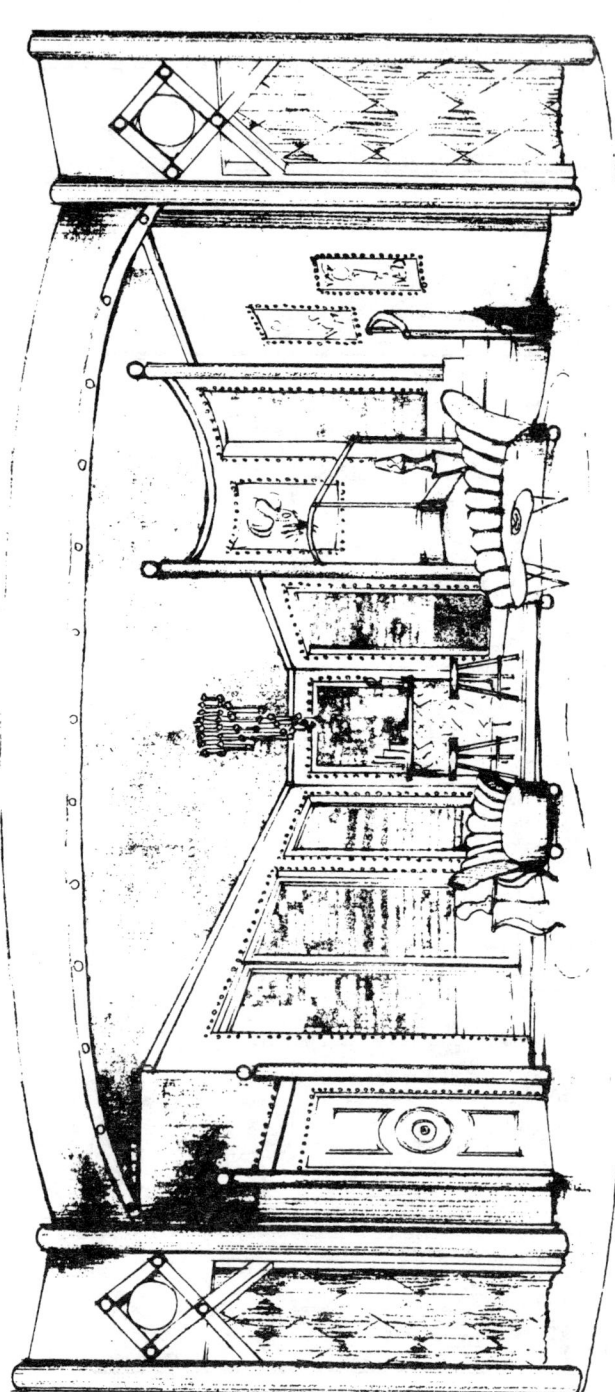

RUTHLESS! ACT II   Lawrence Miller © 1994

These RUTHLESS! scenic designs are for informational purposes only.
License to produce RUTHLESS! does not include permission to use these designs in conjunction with your production.

Ruthless! Set Designs © 1994 Lawrence Miller. All rights reserved.

NEW FROM SAMUEL FRENCH, INC.

SMOKE ON THE MOUNTAIN
Musical
All Groups

Book by Constance Ray. Conceived by Alan Bailey. Music & lyrics by various authors. 4m., 3f. Int. setting. Imagine a combination of *Pump Boys and Dinettes* and *Talking With* if you want to know about this daffy, delightful new show. We are at the Mt. Pleasant (North Carolina) Baptist Church in 1938, at a Saturday Night Gospel Sing arranged by Pastor Mervin Oglethorpe, a young and enthusiastic minister who also works part time in the local pickle factory, who very cautiously wants to bring his congregation into the "modern world" by (gasp!) having a concert in church! Clearly, many of the, shall we say, "less-square" members of the congregation (us in the audience) think this is a swell idea; but not Miss Maude and Miss Myrtle, two elderly spinsters who are the church's chief benefactors, who are in attendance to make sure nobody enjoys themselves. The evening's entertainment is provided by the Sanders Family Gospel Singers, who perform a slew of standard bluegrass gospel songs, from "Church in the Wildwood" to "I'm Using My Bible As a Roadmap." Between songs, the family members "witness" by telling personal stories—some quirkily humorous and others downright moving—that relate to their trials of faith. A huge success at the McCarter Theatre in Princeton (where it won over even our cynical Editor), *Smoke on the Mountain* was subsequently successfully produced in New York by the Lambs Theatre. "Wildly funny . . . so well-written is this [show] that, instead of laughing at it, I found myself laughing with it, rooting for the family, and singing along and clapping with the rest of the audience. *Smoke on the Mountain* reaches out and grabs you."—The Trentonian. "Exhilarating! A rollicking blend of monologues and musical numbers that adds up to a compone *Chorus Line*."—Variety. "A sophisticated audience went simply wild over *Smoke on the Mountain*."—Philadelphia Daily News. "A charming and funny celebration of Americana. With its mixture of softened cracker-barrel humor, Christian sweetness and light, and its attitude of gentle amusement at the squareness of it all, *Smoke on the Mountain* creates the same mood, at once sentimental and whimsical, [as] *Pump Boys and Dinettes*."—N.Y. Times. (#21236)

FAVORITE MUSICALS *from*

"The House of Plays"

A FINE AND PRIVATE PLACE

(**All Groups**) Book & Lyrics by Erik Haagensen. Music by Richard Isen. Adapted from the novel by Peter S. Beagle. 3m., 2f, (may be played by 2m., 2f.) + 1 raven (may be either m. or f.) Ext. setting. "The grave's a fine and private place./But none, I think, do there embrace." Little did you know, Andrew Marvell, that someday, someone would come up with a charming love story, set in a graveyard, about two lost souls who are buried there, who meet and fall in love. Also inhabiting the cemetery is an eccentric old man who has the gift of being able to see and converse with the inhabitants of the graves, as well as with a raven who swoops in at mealtimes with some dinner he has swiped for the old guy. Also present from time to time is a delightful old Jewish widow, whose husband Morris is buried in the cemetery. She often stops by to tell Morris what's new. Her name is Gertrude, and it is soon apparent that she also stops by to flirt with old Jonathan Rebeck (she doesn't know he actually *lives* there). A crisis arises when it appears the young couple will be separated. The young man, it seems, has been deemed a suicide and, as such, he must be removed from consecrated ground. Their only hope is Jonathan; but to help them Jonathan must come out in the open. Had we but world enough, and time, we would tell you how Jonathan manages to salvage the romance; but we'll just have to hope the above story intrigues you enough to examine the delightful libretto and wonderfully tuneful music for yourself. A sell-out, smash hit at the Goodspeed in Connecticut and, later, at the American Stage Co. in New Jersey (the professional theatre which premiered *Other People's Money*), this happy, whimsical, sentimental, up-beat new show will delight audiences of all ages. . **(#8154)**

Other Publications for Your Interest

MAIL
(ADVANCED GROUPS—MUSICAL)

Book & Lyrics by JERRY COLKER
Music by MICHAEL RUPERS

9 men, 6 women—2 Sets

What a terrific idea for a "concept musical"! As *Mail* opens Alex, an unpublished novelist, is having an acute anxiety attack over his lack of success in writing and his indecision regarding his girlfriend, Dana; so, he "hits the ground running" and doesn't come back for 4 months! When Alex finally returns to his apartment, he finds an unending stream of messages on his answering machine and stacks and stacks of unopened mail. As he opens his mail, it in effect comes to life, as we learn what has been happening with Alex's friends, and with Dana, during his absence. There is also some hilarious junk mail, which bombards Alex musically, as well as unpaid bills from the likes of the electric company (the ensemble comes dancing out of Alex's refrigerator singing "We're Gonna Turn Off Your Juice"). In the second act, we move into a sort of abstract vision of Alex's world, a blank piece of paper upon which he can, if he is able, and if he wishes, start over—with his writing, with his friends, with his father and, maybe, with Dana. Producers looking for something wild and crazy will, we know, want to open *this* MAIL, a hit with audiences and critics coast-to-coast, from the authors of THREE GUYS NAKED FROM THE WAIST DOWN! "At least 12 songs are solid enough to stand on their own. If MAIL can't deliver, there is little hope for the future of the musical theatre, unless we continue to rely on the British to take possession of a truly American art form."—Drama-Logue. "Make room for the theatre's newest musical geniuses."—The Same. (Terms quoted on application. Music available on rental. See p. 48.)

(#15199)

CHESS
(ADVANCED GROUPS—MUSICAL/OPERA)

Book by RICHARD NELSON
Lyrics by TIM RICE
Music by BJORN ULVAEUS & BENNY ANDERSSON

9 men, 2 women, 1 female child, plus ensemble

A *musical* about an *international chess match?!?!* A bad idea from the get-go, you'd think; but no—Tim Rice (he of *Evita, Joseph and the Amazing Technicolor Dreamcoat* and *Jesus Christ Superstar*), Bjorn Ulvaeus and Benny Andersson (they of Swedish Supergroup ABBA) and noted American playwright Richard Nelson, all in collaboration with Trevor Nunn (*Les Miz., Nick Nick*, etc.) have pulled it off, creating an extraordinary rock opera about international intrigue which uses as a metaphor a media-drenched chess match between a loutish American champion (shades of Bobby Fischer) and a nice-guy Soviet champion. The American has a girlfriend, Florence, there in Bangkok (where the match takes place) to be his second and to provide moral support. There she meets, and falls in love with, Anatoly, the Soviet champion—and the sparks fly, particularly when Anatoly decides to defect to the west, causing a postponement and change of venue to Budapest. Eventually, it is clear that all the characters are merely pawns in a larger chess match between the C.I.A. and the KGB! The pivotal role of Florence is perhaps the most extraordinary and complex role in the musical theatre since Eva Peron; and the roles of Freddie and Anatoly (both tenors) are great, too. Several of the songs have become international hits, including Florence's "Heaven Help My Heart", "I know Him So Well" and "Nobody's On Nobody's Side", and Freddie's descent into the maelstrom of decadence, "One Night in Bangkok". Playing to full houses and standing ovations, *Chess* closed exceedingly prematurely on Broadway; and, perhaps the story behind *that* just might make the basis of another Rice/ABBA/Nelson/Nunn collaboration! (Terms quoted on application. Music available on rental. See p. 48.) Slightly restricted.

(#5236)

NEW MUSICALS
from
THE HOUSE OF PLAYS

THE ACT—ANGRY HOUSEWIVES—CLASS MUSICAL!—DIAMONDS—DO BLACK PATENT LEATHER SHOES REALLY REFLECT UP?—DOONESBURY—FIRST TIME—THE FRANKENSTEIN MONSTER SHOW—THE GIFT OF THE MAGI—GOODTIME CHARLEY—HAMLET CHA-CHA-CHA—HARRIGAN 'N HART—THE HIGH LIFE—HOW TO EAT LIKE A CHILD—JERRY'S GIRLS—JUST SO—KUNI-LEML—LA CAGE AUX FOLLES—LADY DAY AT EMERSON'S BAR AND GRILL—LEADER OF THE PACK—LOVE WITH A TWIST—MAYOR—NUNSENSE—OLYMPUS ON MY MIND—ONE MO' TIME—PERSONALS—THE RISE OF DAVID LEVINSKY—SMIKE—SMILE—STARDUST—THE TAP DANCE KID—THREE GUYS NAKED FROM THE WAIST DOWN—TO WHOM IT MAY CONCERN—THE WOMAN IN WHITE

For descriptions of all our musicals, consult our Musicals Catalogue — available FREE!!!